New Edition

Artificial Intelligence

8

TEXTBOOK

(As per CBSE Syllabus Code 417)

Authors
Harmeet Kaur
Sangita Chadha

bpb

FIRST EDITION 2020

REPRINT 2025

ISBN: 978-93-89845-068

Distributors:

BPB PUBLICATIONS

20, Ansari Road, Darya Ganj

New Delhi-110002

Ph: 23254990/23254991

DECCAN AGENCIES

4-3-329, Bank Street,

Hyderabad-500195

Ph: 24756967/24756400

MICRO MEDIA

Shop No. 5, Mahendra Chambers,

150 DN Rd. Next to Capital Cinema,

V.T. (C.S.T.) Station, MUMBAI-400 001

Ph: 22078296/22078297

BPB BOOK CENTRE

376 Old Lajpat Rai Market,

Delhi-110006

Ph: 23861747

Published by Manish Jain for BPB Publications, 20 Ansari Road, Darya Ganj, New Delhi-110002 and Printed at Repro India Ltd, Mumbai

Dedicated to

Our parents, family members, peers

and dear students

About the Authors

Harmeet Kaur is currently working as Senior Computer Teacher, Department of Computer Science at Heritage Xperiential Learning School, Gurugram. She has over 21 years of experience in the field of education; teaching Computer Science, Informatics Practices and Multimedia and Web Technologies to grades XI and XII along with a background of mentoring, IT curriculum development for STEM integration, and staff training and development. She has led various in-house projects such as Learning Management System to propagate collaborative personalized e-Learning. She is well adept in Google Apps for Education and uses it as a primary platform for her classroom teaching. She integrates multiple teaching styles to build digital literacy skills in millennial learners while strongly promoting safe and ethical use of technology. She believes in driving the experiential and project-based pedagogy by imparting mobile computing skills to high school students. She has conducted various workshops in and around Delhi-NCR to train teachers with latest pedagogies of classroom management, incorporating Tech to teach STEM education and "learning by doing" hands-on workshops. She has authored training material for in-house teacher training and been constructive in ICT curriculum development.

Sangita Chadha has been working as Head of Computer Department in Ambience Public School, Safdarjung Enclave, New Delhi from last 12 years. She has over twenty years of experience in the field of education; teaching Computer Science, Informatics Practices and Multimedia & Web Technology to grades XI and XII; and has been multifold responsibilities at her school (Result In-charge, ERP, Website, Almanac, Magazine). She is a passionate learner and committed educator consistently working to make learning enjoyable for the learners. Her foremost classroom pedagogy is centered around project-based learning. She has conducted ICT and Net safety workshops for all stakeholders. She has been part of the curriculum development team for classes IX and X Information and Communication Technology, NCERT. She has co-authored class IX and X ICT for NCERT. She also co-authored Class XII Informatics Practices and Computer Science, NCERT. She has conducted Teacher Training workshops for SCERT Teachers.

About the Reviewer

Rekha Verma is a 1st class MCA degree holder and has a teaching experience of 19 years, with a strong command of Python, C++, Java and current software. She had received recommendation letters from HRD Minister-Smriti Irani for board results.

Acknowledgements

We would like to acknowledge the contributions of all the educators, data scientists, scientists, professionals from various fields for their valuable suggestions in developing the content for this book.

We would like to express our gratitude to everyone at BPB Publications for giving us this opportunity to write the book. We are thankful to all the resource persons at BPB Publications for editing, technical reviewing and language editing the book. We would like to thank our technical reviewer, Mrs. Rekha Verma for her thoughtful insights while refining the manuscript of this book.

We are thankful to each other and our families for being supportive in numerous ways and for giving their unconditional love and support at all times.

Lastly, but not the least, we would like to thank God for bearing us with courage and humility to be able to write this book for our students.

— Harmeet Kaur

— Sangita Chadha

Preface

Artificial Intelligence is a growing and important field in Computer Science. AI has become very popular in today's times. The goals of scientists in recent times have been to create technology to allow computers to be able to take human-like smart decisions and behave in intelligent manner. AI has become a prevalent jargon due to increasing dependency on Big Data; algorithms working on the bulk of data collection and improving capabilities in computing and storage. It is impacting the life of everyone in the field of education, entertainment, transport, and many more.

Artificial Intelligence is an important aspect of policy decision makers in many countries. In India, the lawmakers have been focusing on including AI in multiple fields to propagate economic growth. The impact of AI is visible in multiple arenas affecting the young and old in a similar manner. The understanding of Artificial Intelligence is very crucial in the deployment of various solutions proliferating sustainable development goals in today's times.

The primary objective in the development of this book is to create a pedagogical approach that emphasizes on the basic concepts of Artificial Intelligence. This book contains many examples to make the student learn, understand about various domains of Artificial Intelligence easily using various activities. Each activity is connected with real life scenario to make the learner connected with the world and become a global citizen. Learners understand the simulations in real time. They are even able to develop some of the simulations without knowing the programming language and hence, efficiently employ the potentials of AI in a viable manner.

This book is divided into 5 chapters and it provides a detailed description of the basic concepts of Artificial Intelligence.

Chapter 1 excites the learners to explore and get motivated about Artificial Intelligence applications in their daily lives. The chapter entails multiple gaming activities to make them understand the three pillars of AI (Data for Artificial Intelligence, Natural Language Processing and Computer Vision). The chapter clearly explains the rules for all gaming activities with individualistic learning being encouraged while practicing critical thinking skills.

Chapter 2 contains web accessible resources for the learner to recognize the areas where Artificial Intelligence plays significant applicability in their lives. They are able to foresee their expectations for future AI readiness and devise plans with the information collected. The chapter ends with the steps to create an interactive story around futuristic homes by means of which the learner gains the skill of applying and reflecting on human-machine expectations.

Chapter 3 clearly earmarks the 17 Sustainable Development Goals for the learner to be able to understand, summarize and relate with while listing the societal issues where Artificial Intelligence can have major implications. The learner is able to determine the Artificial Intelligence solutions which would be appropriate to solve the said goals. The chapter ends with strategy for conversational discussions to enlighten the learner to appreciate the complexity of social issues and leverage points to achieve them through Artificial Intelligence.

Chapter 4 exclusively specifies strategies for the learner to be able to paraphrase their theme-based research of various case studies and develop awareness of skills required for jobs of the future. The learners will explore the emergence of Artificial Intelligence jobs in various fields and their impact on future. Skills such as communication and collaborative skills are honed while learning how to design activities for finalizing the skill sets for future jobs.

Chapter 5 focuses on empowering the learner to understand and reflect on the ethical issues around Artificial Intelligence and critically evaluate the cost and benefits of Artificial Intelligence technology. Further, the chapter clearly enumerates how to compare and contrast the societal advantages and disadvantages of Artificial Intelligence inclusion.

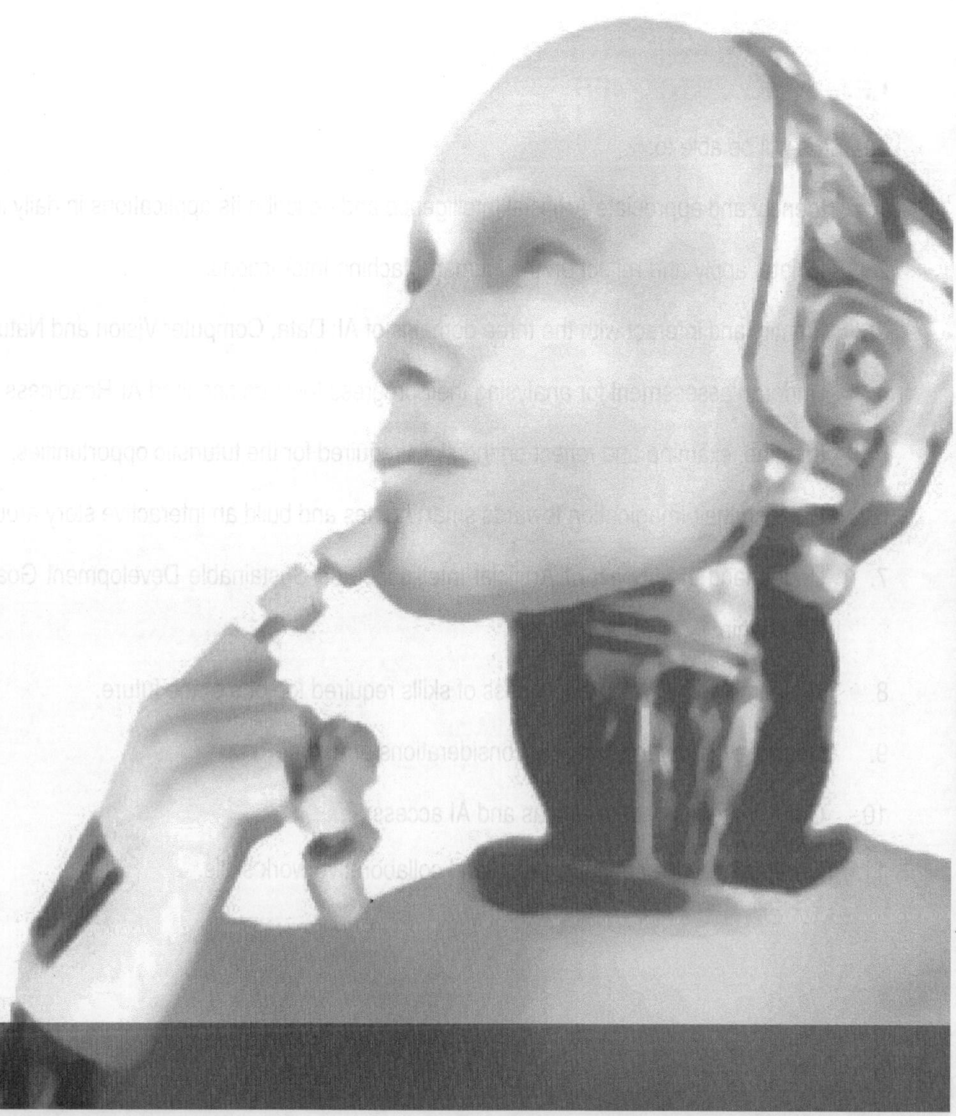

SYLLABUS

OBJECTIVE

The objective of this module/curriculum is to develop a readiness for understanding and appreciating Artificial Intelligence and its application in our lives.

This module/ curriculum focuses on:

1. Helping learners understand the world of Artificial Intelligence and its applications through games, activities and multi-sensorial learning to become AI-Ready.
2. Introducing the learners to three domains of AI in an age appropriate manner.
3. Allowing the learners to construct meaning of AI through interactive participationand engaging hands-on activities.

LEARNING OUTCOMES

Learners will be able to:

1. Identify and appreciate Artificial Intelligence and describe its applications in daily life.
2. Relate, apply and reflect on the Human-Machine Interactions.
3. Identify and interact with the three domains of AI: Data, Computer Vision and Natural Language Processing.
4. Undergo assessment for analysing their progress towards acquired AI-Readiness skills.
5. Imagine, examine and reflect on the skills required for the futuristic opportunities.
6. Unleash their imagination towards smart homes and build an interactive story around it.
7. Understand the impact of Artificial Intelligence on Sustainable Development Goals to develop responsible citizenship.
8. Research and develop awareness of skills required for jobs of the future.
9. Describe the potential ethical considerations of AI.
10. Gain awareness about AI bias and AI access.
11. Develop effective communication and collaborative work skills.

UNIT WISE DISTRIBUTION

UNIT	NAME OF THE UNIT	DURATION	PERIODS
1	EXCITE	02 Hours 40 Mins.	4 Periods
2	RELATE	02 Hours	3 Periods
3	PURPOSE	02 Hours	3 Periods
4	POSSIBILITIES	02 Hours	3 Periods
5	AI ETHICS	03 Hours 20 Mins.	5 Periods
	TOTAL	12 Hours	18 Periods

COURSE OUTLINE

UNIT (INSPIRE)	ACTIVITY/SESSION	LEARNING OUTCOMES
1. EXCITE	Session: Introduction to AI and setting up the context of the curriculum. Ice Breaker Activity: Dream Smart Home idea Learners to design a rough layout of floor plan of their dream Smart Home.	To identify and appreciate Artificial Intelligence and describe its applications in daily life.
	Recommended Activity: The AI Game Learners to participate in three games based on different AI domains. • Game 1: Rock, Paper and Scissors (based on data) • Game 2: Mystery Animal (based on Natural Language Processing - NLP) • Game 3: Emoji Scavenger Hunt (based on Computer Vision - CV)	To relate, apply and reflect on the Human-Machine Interactions. To identify and interact with the three domains of AI: Data, Computer Vision and Natural Language Processing.
	Recommended Activity: AI Quiz (Paper Pen/Online Quiz) Recommended Activity: To write a letter Writing a Letter to one's future self. Learners to write a letter to self-keeping the future in context. They will describe what they have learnt so far or what thcy would lIke to learn someday	To undergo an assessment for analysing progress towards acquired AI-Readiness skills. To imagine, examine and reflect on the skills required for the futuristic opportunities.

<table>
<tr><td rowspan="2">2. RELATE</td><td>Video Session: To watch a video Introducing the concept of Smart Cities, Smart Schools and Smart Homes.</td><td>Learners to relate to application of Artificial Intelligence in their daily lives.</td></tr>
<tr><td>Recommended Activity:
To write an Interactive Story Learners to draw a floor plan of a Home/School/City and write an interactive story around it using Story Speaker extension in Google docs.</td><td>To unleash their imagination towards Smart Homes and build an interactive story around it.
To relate, apply and reflect on the Human-Machine Interactions.</td></tr>
<tr><td rowspan="2">3. PURPOSE</td><td>Session: Introduction to Sustainable Development Goals.</td><td rowspan="2">To understand the impact of Artificial Intelligence on Sustainable Development Goals to develop responsible citizenship.</td></tr>
<tr><td>Recommended Activity: Go Goals Board Game
• Learners to answer questionson Sustainable Development Goals.</td></tr>
<tr><td rowspan="2">4. POSSIBILITIES</td><td>Session: Theme-based research and case studies
• Learners will listen to various case-studies of inspiring start-ups, companies or communities where AI has been involved in real-life.
• Learners will be allotted a theme around which they need to search for present AI trends and have to visualise the future of AI in and around their respective theme.</td><td rowspan="2">To research and develop awareness of skills required for jobs of the future.
To imagine, examine and reflect on the skills required for the futuristic opportunities.
To develop effective communication and collaborative work skills.</td></tr>
<tr><td>Recommended Activity: Job Ad Creating activity
• Learners to create a job advertisement for a firm describing the nature of job available and the skill-set required for it 10 years down the line. They need to figure out how AI is going to transform the nature of jobs and create the Ad accordingly.</td></tr>
</table>

5.AI ETHICS	**Video Session:** Discussing about AI Ethics	To understand and reflect on the ethical issues around AI.
	Recommended Activity: Ethics Awareness • Students play the role of major stakeholders and they have to decide what is ethical and what is not for a given scenario.	
	Session: AI Bias and AI Access • Discussing about the possible bias in data collection. • Discussing about the implications of AI technology.	To gain awareness around AI bias and AI access.
	Recommended Activity: Balloon Debate • Students divide in teams of 3 and 2 teams are given same theme. One team goes in affirmation to AI for their section while the other one goes against it. • They have to come up with their points as to why AI is beneficial/harmful for the society.	To let the students analyse the advantages and disadvantages of Artificial Intelligence.

Contents

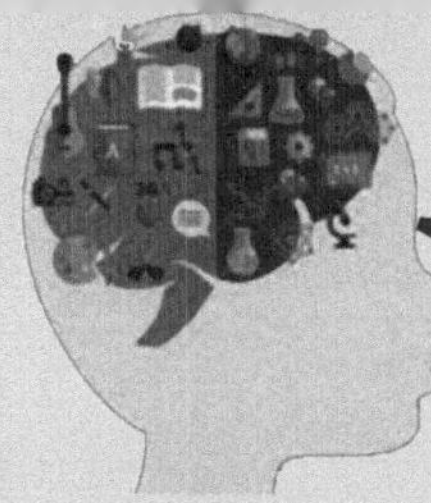

1 Motivate with AI

Structure Bot

In this chapter, we will discuss the following topics:

- Meaning of the term Artificial Intelligence
- Applications of Artificial Intelligence in your daily lives
- Three domains of Artificial Intelligence
  - Data for Artificial Intelligence
  - Natural Language Processing
  - Computer Vision

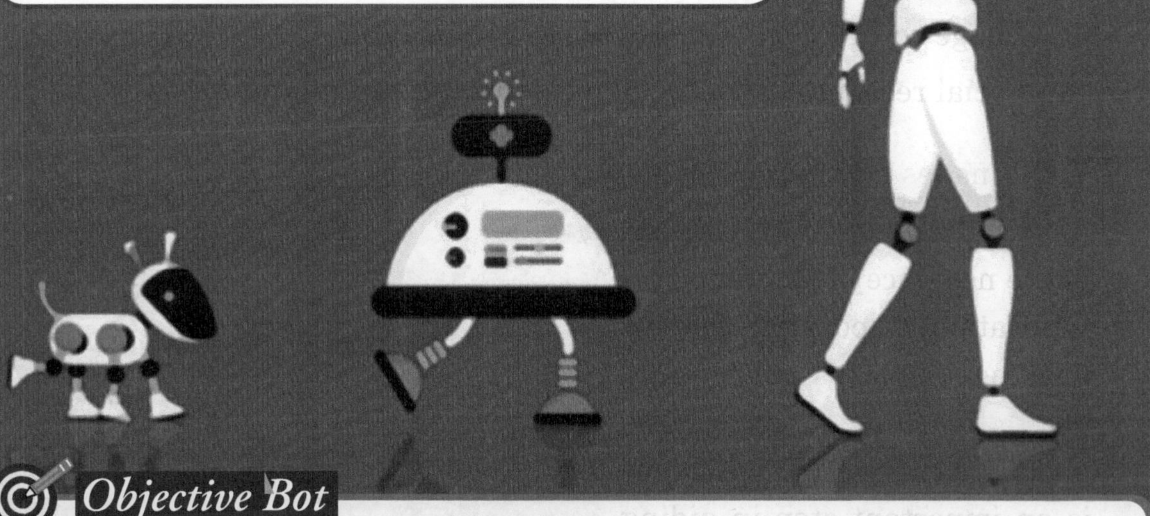

Objective Bot

At the end of this chapter, you should be able to:

- Understand the concept of Artificial Intelligence
- Demonstrate/discuss/elaborate the use of AI applications in your daily lives
- Determine the type of domains used in various AI applications
- Interact and explain the use of AI domains in various applications
- Learn to relate with Artificial Intelligence Domains, namely, Data for Artificial Intelligence, Natural Language Processing, and Computer Vision

What is Artificial Intelligence?

Let's start by asking a few questions.

1. What things are easy for computers to do that are hard for humans?
   a. Math problems such as adding/multiplying/dividing.
   b. Searching for an item from a list.
   c. Sorting items based on a particular attribute (numbers, letters, words, and so on).

2. What tasks are easy for humans to do that are hard for computers?
   a. Voice recognition: Sarcasm (emotion).
   b. Voice recognition: The context and semantics of language.
   c. Image recognition: Finding objects in images.
   d. Facial recognition: Recognizing someone in a photo.

3. What makes a human intelligent?

Artificial Intelligence, or 'AI', is the new face of technological innovation responsible for the new age changes all around us. Teaching awareness about Artificial Intelligence is an important step in aiding today's generation to comprehend the restrictions, challenges, prospects, ethics, and menaces of using technology. Along the same lines, it is equally necessary to be able to create technological solutions using elements of AI to new modernizations.

Figure 1.1: *Artificial Intelligence*

Artificial Intelligence (AI) was first coined in 1956 by a cognitive scientist, John McCarthy, at the Dartmouth Conference—the first Artificial Intelligence conference. The main thought behind the project was to explore ways to make a machine that could reason like a human, was capable of abstract thought, problem-solving and self-improvement. Artificial Intelligence is the creation of machines to impersonate human capabilities such as teaching a machine to be able to distinguish objects in an image and to listen, deduce, and evaluate sounds.

Definition Bot

Artificial intelligence (AI) refers to the simulation of intelligent behaviour in computer.

There are multiple areas where AI has made a lot of progress in the past years. AI systems have been used across areas creating solutions for individuals and society. Four main areas where AI has made the most possible advancements till date are as follows:

- To see
- To communicate
- To move
- To think

Self-driving vehicles are cars or trucks in which human drivers are never required to take control to safely operate the vehicle. Also known as autonomous or driverless cars, they combine sensors and software to control, navigate, and drive the vehicle.

Figure 1.2: *Waymo: driverless car*

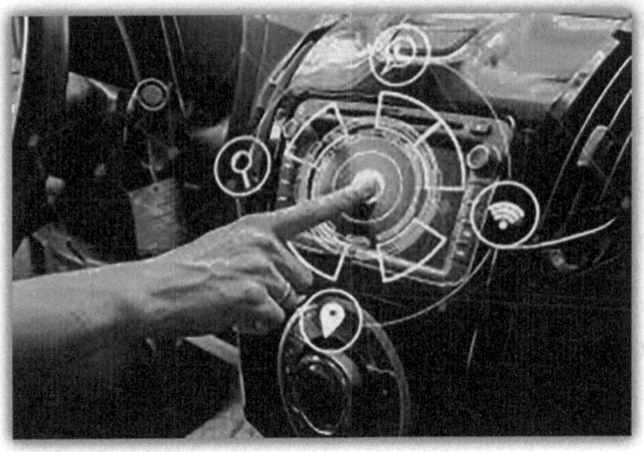

Figure 1.3: *AI in transport*

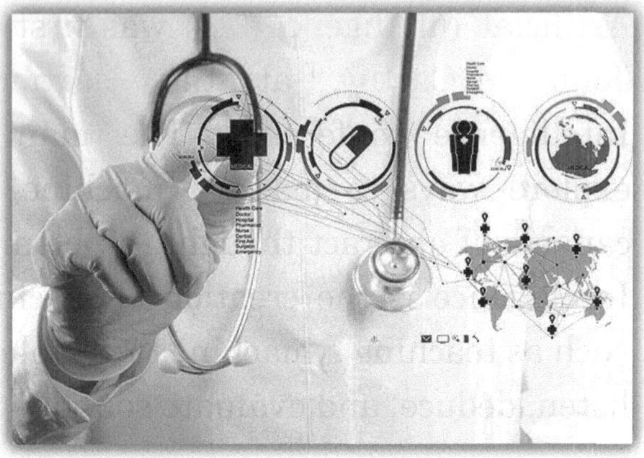

Figure 1.4: *AI in healthcare*

The AI app is one of the many apps that has several provisions that communicate with other technologies which are useful to users with visual impairments. AI expanded microscopes are used by pathologists for real-time detection of cancer, thus saving patients' lives. AI supported apps can even help people with visual impairments to use the touch feature of the app to explore the objects and people in photos based on data generated by converting visual data into audio feedback. In recent developments, a team of international astronomers captured an image of a black hole's silhouette by creating a network of telescopes known as the Event Horizon Telescope. There are multiple language translators available online which assist in communication. There are many online portals available which help us in learning the language online. Such users help in improvement of AI associated with translating languages.

Figure 1.5: *AI in food production*

Recent technologies such as Siri, Google Assistant, Alexa, AI-based chatbots, and so on provide interactions using Natural Language

KNOWLEDGE BOT

AI devices can be setup at places where it is difficult for human to live.

Processing in interpreting user questions providing meaningful solutions and information such as news, weather, time, and directions. Very recently, Harish Natarajan who holds the world record for the highest number of international debate victories was served a convincing argument by IBM's Project Debater about a given topic which it had not been programmed to learn. This was the first time an AI machine was able to do so.

Figure 1.6: *AI device - Alexo*

Figure 1.7: *AI device - Cortana*

AI systems are also capable to think based on logic-based and pattern matching algorithms to beat humans in games like chess. Two examples are IBM's Deep Blue, which holds the record of beating the World Chess Champion in 1997 and Google Deep Mind's Go-playing AI, Alpha-Go defeated the World Champion in 2017. Robotics has made a huge impact using technology where they can learn to perform actions like humans. Assistive robots and drones have been used in search and rescue, bomb squads, and agriculture.

To sum it up, you can easily state a few uses of AI in your everyday life.

1. **Music and Media:** Artificial Intelligence is helping users to find music and media of their choice on apps like Spotify, Netflix, or YouTube. This is done by AI algorithms, which learn about user selections done regularly over a time period and hence provide recommendations to add to one's playlist.

Figure 1.8: *Spotify*

2. **Smart Home Devices:** Artificial Intelligence is used in smart home

devices to adjust the house temperature and lighting based on one's preferences.

Activity 1.1

Let's pen down your thoughts here to understand how AI can help in your daily lives. Also, mention a few areas where AI is used in your daily lives.

1. ______________________
2. ______________________
3. ______________________
4. ______________________
5. ______________________
6. ______________________
7. ______________________

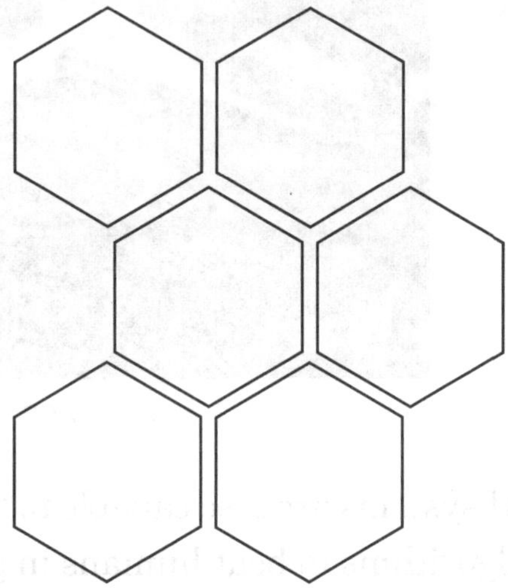

3. **Online services:** Industries ranging from travel to banking, shopping, and entertainment rely heavily on Artificial Intelligence for using chatbots or through algorithms that enable it to track spending, suggest purchases, prevent fraud, and complete other transactions much faster.

4. **Smartphones:** AI integration in mobile technology is bringing features like face detection, virtual reality elements, photo editor, and many more to name some. A huge emphasis on AI is quite evident with the latest Android and iOS updates. Many new features like app actions, splices, and adaptive

Figure 1.9: *Smartphone*

battery in Android Pie and Siri shortcut and Siri suggestions in iOS 12 have been made possible with AI.

5. **Smart Cars:** A huge progress is evidently seen with automatic cars on the road. Tesla cars are a prime example of how the AI is impacting your daily life. An estimated 50,000 Tesla cars are running in the US alone.

6. **Social Media Feeds:** Artificial Intelligence plays a vital role on one's actions on social media apps. The feeds that you see in your timeline along with the notifications that you receive from these apps is curated mainly by AI. A user's past behavior, web searches, interactions; namely, one's Digital Footprint tailors the experience for that user. Such intentions only make the apps so addictive that you come back to them again and again.

7. **Video Games:** Every user that plays a game such as PUBG or Fortnite essentially starts playing against a couple of AI-powered bots and then move to play against real players in consecutive levels. If you are playing racing games, you are racing against AI bots.

8. **Online Ads Network:** The online advertisement industry uses AI to not only track user statistics but also serves user ads based on those statistics. The online ad industry will just fail if it were not relying heavily on the user preferences and past behaviors. It would show random ads to users with no connection to their preferences. The user surveys aid to data collection algorithms which help set the repetition or display of such advertisements online.

9. **Navigation and Travel:** Artificial Intelligence is used to interpret hundreds of thousands of datapoints that they receive with user inputs to suggest real-time traffic data. Google Maps and Waze are one of the few examples along with others which are used for navigation services. While calling an Uber or Ola,

Figure 1.10: *AI in navigation*

both the pricing and the car that matches one's ride request is decided by AI algorithms.

10. **Security and Surveillance:** With latest developments in technologies like object recognition and facial recognition getting better every day, soon all the security camera feeds will be monitored by AI and not a human.

Figure 1.11: *AI in security*

> **TIP BOT**
>
> AI products are being used in many different domains such as banking and finance, healthcare, manufacturing, retail, and so on.

Dream Smart Home

The dream of creating Smart Homes which help us in your every day lives has been made possible with the latest innovations in the field of sensors, neural networks, engineering, and Artificial Intelligence.

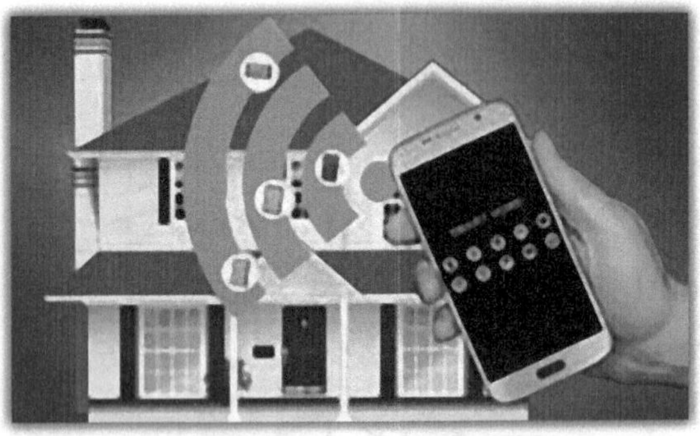

Figure 1.12: *Smart Home*

> **FACT BOT**
>
> - In 1999, Gujarat was the first Indian state to introduce a smart card license system.
> - Russian President, Vladimir Putin, stated that AI is the future and whoever becomes a leader in AI will become the ruler of the world.

Activity 1.2

Let's investigate some of the technologies which might be available to us in the future.

1. Watch the video at https://youtu.be/CPH1sAY8Vhg very carefully and fill the organizer.
2. Identify five different technologies which you saw in the video and expect them to be available at home in the near future.

a. ____________________

b. ____________________

c. ____________________

d. ____________________

e. ____________________

Activity 1.3

Design a Floor Plan of your ideal Smart Home which could have different technologies in the future. Clearly, earmark all rooms, garden, swimming pool, and so on and title them accordingly. Also, list the gadgets which could be in your Smart Home.

List the Smart Gadgets that could be in your Smart Home.

1. ______________________ 5. ______________________

2. ______________________ 6. ______________________

3. ______________________ 7. ______________________

4. ______________________ 8. ______________________

Smart Homes are used for several purposes. They can improve comfort at home, reduce energy consumption, and enable automation of household chores. They can provide a better-quality entertainment by adapting their behaviors to the preferences of residents.

However, many scientists believe that the field of Smart Homes will reach its full potential by providing health assistance to impaired or frail persons and aid in assisted living.

A Floor Plan example can be as follows:

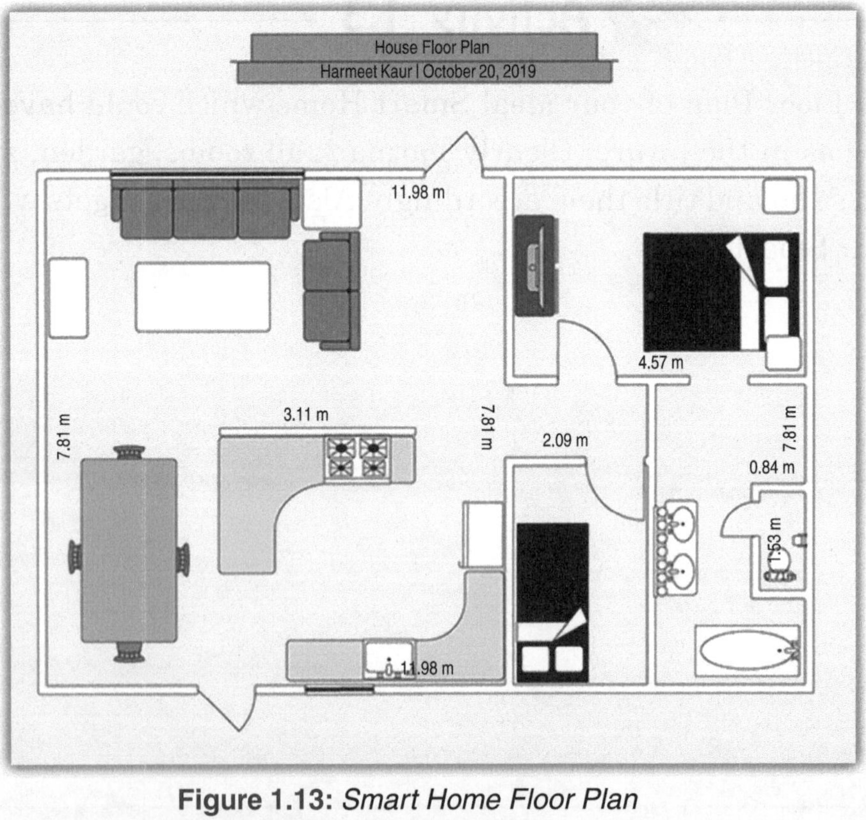

Figure 1.13: *Smart Home Floor Plan*

Gamification

It is the process of adding game-like components to a task so as to encourage user participation. It helps in combining fun with non-game activities to understand a concept better. The process uses data-driven techniques to engage players and motivate learners.

The latest research in AI has focused chiefly on the following components of intelligence learning, cognitive, logic building, observation, analytics, and understanding vocal commands. Fun features such as winning badges and leader boards add an extra edge to the whole learning process.

How is Artificial Intelligence used in Games?

In video games, Artificial Intelligence (AI) is used to generate responsive, adaptive or intelligent behaviors primarily in Non-Player Characters (NPCs) similar to human-like intelligence.

Games play a very important role in your lives. Game-based learning makes students very enthusiastic and it becomes very easy to make them understand the concept. They like to collaborate, communicate, interact, and work in teams. Gaming actually creates the atmosphere that inspires learners to develop skills and build an emotional connect with the subject which is very difficult otherwise.

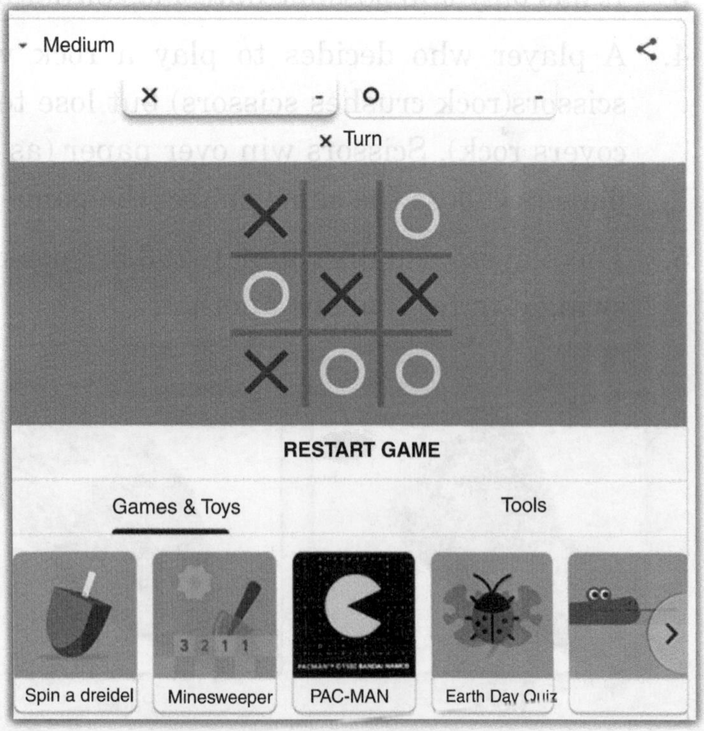

Figure 1.14: *Gamification*

Research has shown that it is very easy to make the student learn by play way method. Each game has the object of the game, players and equipment, scoring, and winning. So, a game has certain set of rules before you start playing.

Game 1: Rock-Paper-Scissors

Let us talk about Rock-Paper-Scissors, which is a hand game. Let us understand some set of rules for the game:

1. You require two players.
2. Each player simultaneously forms one of the three shapes with an out stretched hand.
   a. If you show a flat hand that means a paper.
   b. If you show a closed fist that means a rock, and if you show a fist with the index finger and middle finger extended forming a "V" that means a scissor.
3. It has only two possible outcomes either a draw or a win.
4. A player who decides to play a rock wins over the one who shows scissors(rock crushes scissors) but lose to one who plays a paper (paper covers rock). Scissors win over paper (as scissors cut paper). If both the players choose the same shape, the game is tied.
5. The players usually count 1, 2, 3 or speak Rock, Paper, Scissor, and then swing it in front of one another.

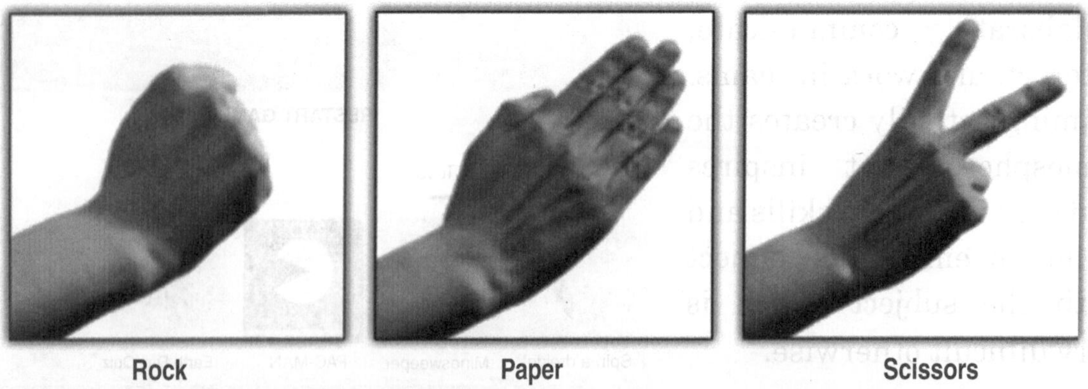

Figure 1.15: *Image representations of game attributes*

Using this game, one player is always trying to predict the next move of another player. Also, remembering the moves and predicting from the previous moves, the game is played.

Activity 1.4

Let us play Rock, Paper, Scissors game on a computer based on data and try to understand how you can play against a computer.

Step 1: Open the link: https://www.afiniti.com/corporate/rockpaper-scissors

Prerequisite to play this game.

Open the link in a web browser on your device.

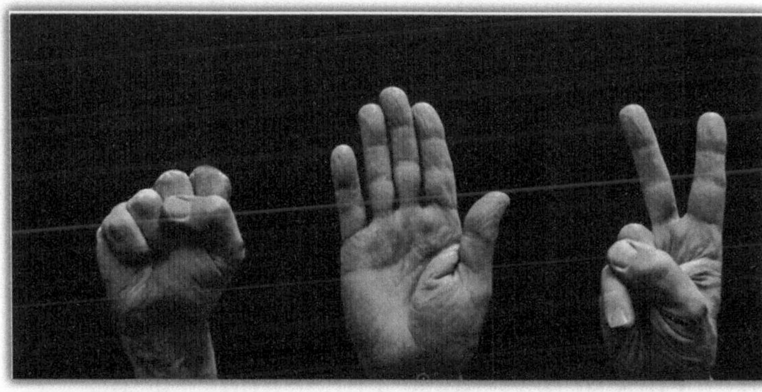

Figure 1.16: *Screenshot image of the game*

Step 2: Click on Play the Game.

Step 3: Click on the Shapes which you want to choose and play against the system. The result will be shown after each move.

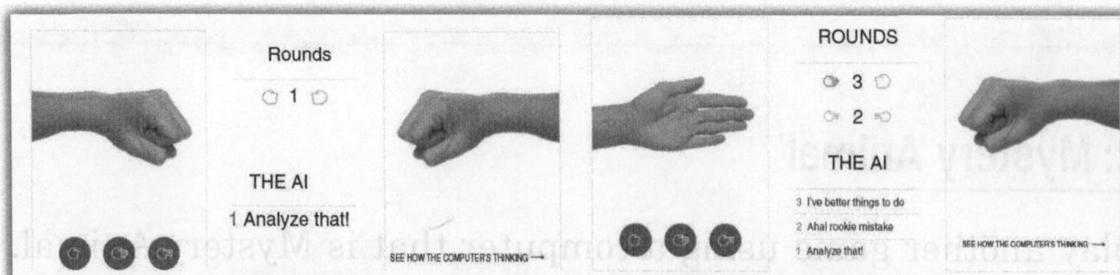

Figure 1.17: *Screenshot of the game in action*

After playing this game, you must have observed that the system is predicting your next move by identifying the patterns of your game behavior. The system is actually analyzing your previous moves' strategy to predict the next move. Therefore, the system is collecting data (that is, your previous moves in this game) and then analyzing it to decide the next move. Collecting data and analyzing it is known as Data for Artificial Intelligence.

Activity 1.5

Write any three things you learned from the game.

1. ______________________________

2. ______________________________

3. ______________________________

Activity 1.6

Write the requirements to play Rock, Paper and Scissor.

1. Internet Connection ______________________________

2. ______________________________

3. ______________________________

Game 2: Mystery Animal

Let us play another game using a computer that is Mystery Animal. Before starting the game, please read the instructions carefully. Let us understand some set of rules for the game:

1. A microphone must be attached to your computer.
2. The participant needs to ask a question to the computer in such a manner that will be answered by the computer in YES or NO form only.
3. The participant gets a chance of asking only 20 questions to decide upon the name of the animal.

Activity 1.7

Let us play the game of Mystery Animal based on Natural Language Processing (NLP).

Step 1: Open the following link in Google chrome browser: https://mysteryanimal.withgoogle.com/

(a)

Step 2: Click on PREVIEW IT HERE and start playing the game.

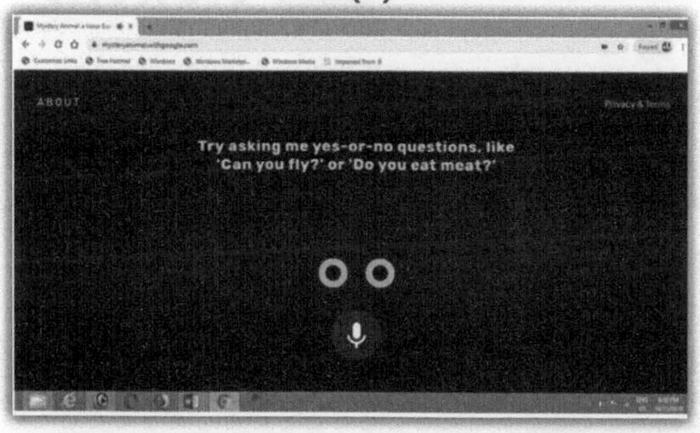

(b)

Step 3: Click on the microphone 🎙 button and start asking a question which has needs to be answered in YES or NO.

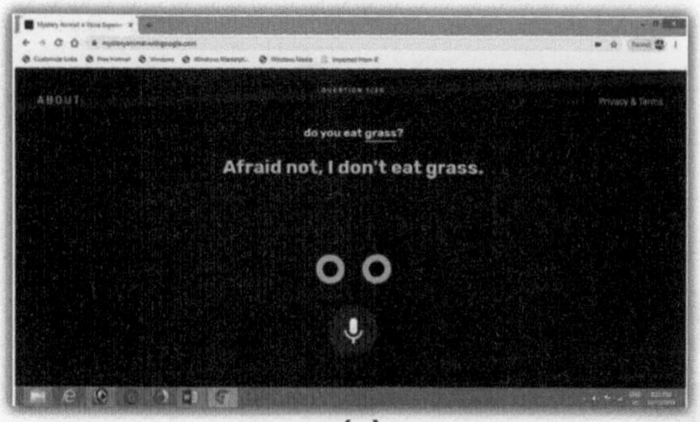

(c)

Figure 1.18: *Screenshot of the game in action*

After playing this game, you must have observed that as you ask a question on the computer's microphone, it gets typed by the computer. Thus, in this game, the computer is processing whatever questions are asked by you. The questions have to be in logical form with either of the answers YES or NO. A maximum of 20 questions can be asked where the animal randomly gets selected for each game by the machine.

Natural Language Processing (NLP)

It is the technology used to aid computers to understand the human's natural language such as English. Processing of the natural language is required when an intelligent machine needs to perform some actions based on instructions given by you.

> **MEMORY BOT**
>
> Natural Language Processing is one of the sub-fields of Artificial Intelligence wherein the machine interprets human language and produces intelligent output.

Activity 1.8

Mention three things you understood about the game.

1. ______________________
2. ______________________
3. ______________________

Activity 1.9

Write the requirements to play Mystery Animal.

1. Internet Connection ______________________
2. ______________________
3. ______________________

Activity 1.10

Let us play the game of Emoji Scavenger Hunt based on Computer Vision.

Step 1: Open the following link in a web browser:
https://emojiscavengerhunt.withgoogle.com/

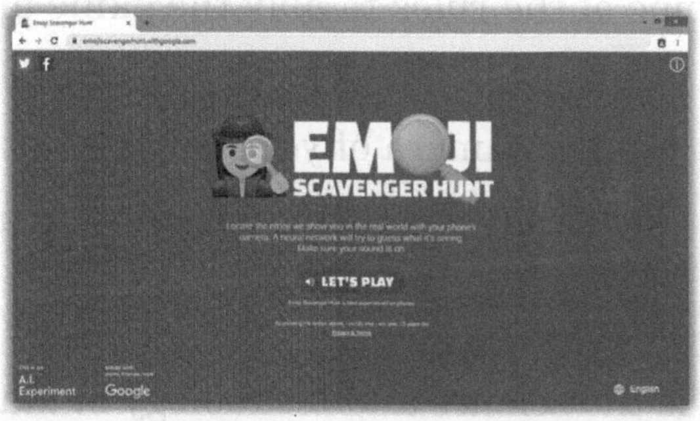

Figure 1.19: *Screenshot of the game in action*

Figure 1.20: *Click on the Allow button to make use of the web camera*

Step 2: Click on Let's Play option.

Step 3: Allow the camera and microphone and then start playing as per the instructions coming on the screen.

Step 4: Show the image on the camera so that it can detect the image and match it with the object asked in the Find. The Find box displays the icon of the image being searched to be shown in the camera.

Emoji Scavenger Hunt is a game based on Computer Vision where the machine initiates the game by showing emoji. The participant is expected to show a similar object in front of the camera while the machine keeps on guessing what is being shown to it.

Figure 1.21: *Show the picture of a book in of the camera front*

Game 3: Emoji Scavenger Hunt

Let us play another game known as Emoji Scavenger on a web browser. Some of the rules to play the game are as follows:

1. A webcam must be attached to your computer or the user can make use of the camera of your Smartphone / tablet.
2. The player must have access to a few of objects used in everyday lives.

Computer Vision

It is the science and technology of machines that see. It is concerned with the theory and technology for building artificial systems that obtain information from images.

Activity 1.11

Did you face any difficulty while playing this game? How did you overcome this?

1. ____________________
2. ____________________
3. ____________________
4. ____________________

Activity 1.12

Write the requirements to play Emoji Scavenger Hunt.

1. Internet Connection ____________________
2. ____________________
3. ____________________
4. ____________________

Food for thought 1

Rock, Paper and Scissors How does the machine react if you: • Move in a specific pattern • Make moves randomly	
Mystery Animal What kind of questions would you ask the computer to figure out the basic characteristics of the animal?	
Emoji Scavenger Hunt How would the machine react if you were to show an emoji drawn on the paper to the machine?	

Practice Time

Answer the following questions.

1. Write down one example of navigation service.
2. What is the use of Smart Home device?
3. Which technology used to aid computers to understand the human's natural language such as English?

Food for thought 2

Activity 1.13

Write a letter to your future self, keeping the following points in mind.

1. Mention what you have learned about Artificial Intelligence.
2. Mention the skills you would like to learn and acquire for availing future jobs.

Solution: Letter to Future Self

Hello My Future Self,

Artificial Intelligence is combining intelligence with artificial devices. Artificial Intelligence refers to computer systems with combination of hardware and software that are capable of performing special tasks such as recognizing multimedia such as images, videos, speech, etc. which influence decision making and strategic planning.

An efficient AI computer system is capable of carrying out behavioral tasks that require humans to use their common intelligence. Representation of facts and information, learning problem solving skills, detailed perceptions with reasoning, enhancing creativity and understanding net etiquettes, and social intelligence are primary skills required for understanding Artificial Intelligence.

Artificial Intelligence makes the machine behave like humans. It allows the machine to imitate human cognitive processes which includes seeing around, learning from experiences and patterns, and process the language to understand and perform an action. Most AI examples that you hear about today from chess-playing computers to self-driving cars – rely collecting data for machine, Computer Vision, and Natural Language Processing. Using these technologies, computers can be trained to accomplish specific tasks by collecting and processing large amount of data and recognizing patterns in the data either using natural language or from Computer Vision. The job opportunities scenario will be changing with the demand for specific jobs in different industries in our future years. The situations are going to create a huge shortage of individual trained in specific areas. The most important areas of AI career jobs will be two faced; developing and deploying AI and Operating AI computer systems.

So, I would like you to be conscientious in your efforts and keep yourself updated with AI future readiness skills for futuristic opportunities.

All the best!!
Your Present Self

Activity 1.14

This is an open-ended activity. The above mentioned activities are that of the authors. You should try to express your understandings and views for the same activity. Write a letter to your future self, keeping the following points in mind.

1. **Mention what you have learned about Artificial Intelligence.**
2. **Mention the skills you would like to learn and acquire for availing future jobs.**
3. **Mention the AI integration in multiple career options that shall require technical skills in future jobs.**

TECH BOT

- **Artificial Intelligence:** It is defined as the simulation of human intelligence by machines, which are programmed to think like human and copy their action.
- **Natural Language Programming (NLP):** It is the ability of a program to understand human language.
- **Smart Home:** It is a home that can be managed remotely to control the items/appliances/gadgets/systems such as TV, AC, fridge, and so on, with your device.

Recap Bot

- The main goal of Artificial Intelligence is to make the machine behave intelligently by seeing, moving, thinking, and communicating.
- The three pillars of Artificial Intelligence are Data for AI, Natural Language Processing and Computer Vision.
- Data for AI in machine is used to predict the next move of human from previous moves collected by the machine.
- Natural Language Processing is a technology with which the machine is able to understand human language such as English and perform an action based on the command.
- Computer Vision is a technology with which the machine can see around and also collect information from images.
- Rock Paper Scissor, Mystery Animal, and Scavenger Hunt are games developed by Google powered by AI to understand the domains of AI.
- Chatbot is an Artificial Intelligence software that can simulate a conversation with users in Natural Language Processing.
- Many AI-based techniques such as Siri, Google Assistant, Alexa, and chatbots are capable of having conversation with a human in real time using NLP. They primarily work on two techniques such as speech recognition and Natural Language Processing.
- The research in the field of Artificial Intelligence is based mainly on learning, cognitive, logic building, observation, analytics, and understanding vocal commands.
- Examples of AI can be seen in smartphones, Smart Cars, drones, social media feeds, and music and media streaming, video games, online advertisements, navigation, travel and tourism, banking, finance management, smart home gadgets, security and surveillance.
- Alan Turing was a computer scientist and cryptanalyst who founded the Turing test, which is used to check whether or not a machine is capable of thinking like a human being.

BRAIN BOT

A. Multiple choice questions.

1. Artificial Intelligence means:
   a. Programming with your own intelligence
   b. Making a machine intelligent
   c. Playing a game with machine
   d. Putting your intelligence in a computer
2. What is the primary method for communication between humans?
   a. Reading b. Writing
   c. Speaking d. All of the above
3. This is a system of programs and data structures that approximates the operation of the human brain.
   a. Intelligent network b. Neural network
   c. Genetic programming d. Decision support system
4. This is the tendency for people to think of in animate objects as having human-like characteristics.
   a. Personalization b. Aliasing
   c. Self-replication d. Anthropomorphism
5. Artificial Intelligence was first coined in 1956 by a cognitive scientist named:
   a. Dr. Lofti Zadeh b. John McCarthy
   c. Alain Colmerauer d. Seymour Papert
6. The AI domain that is capable of communication between people and machines is:
   a. Robotics
   b. Decision support
   c. Computer Vision
   d. Natural Language Processing
7. This is an AI software/program that simulates a conversation with a human being:
   a. Chatbot b. Voice recognition
   c. Speech application d. Data for AI

8. The full form of NLP is:
   a. Neuro-Language Programming
   b. Natural Language Programming
   c. Natural Language Processing
   d. Natural Language Presentation
9. Which generation of computers is associated with Artificial Intelligence?
   a. Fifth b. Fourth
   c. Third d. Second
10. What is the study of how the language sounds?
   a. Speechology b. Trilogy
   c. Biology d. Phonology

B. Fill in the blanks.

1. Artificial Intelligence covers a broad range of ____________.
2. Computer Vision is the technology of machines that can ____________.
3. ____________ is a game based on data for AI.
4. ____________ have made a huge impact using technology where they can learn to perform actions like humans.
5. Assistive robots and ____________ have been used in search and rescue, bomb squads and agriculture.
6. AI systems are capable to think based on logic-based and ____________matching algorithms.

C. Match the following columns.

	Column A		Column B
1.	Chatbots	i.	Python, Lisp
2.	Applications of AI	ii.	NLP
3.	Mystery Animal	iii.	Siri, Alexa
4.	Programming language used in AI	iv.	Computer Vision
5.	Emoji Scavenger Hunt	v.	Self-driving cars, chatbots

D. Answer the following questions.

1. What is Artificial Intelligence? Give a few examples of AI used in your daily life.
2. Write a definition for the following.
   a. NLP
   b. Computer Vision
   c. Data for AI
   d. Gamification
3. Name the three domains of Artificial Intelligence.
4. Name any game where the computer predicts your next move by analysing your previous moves.
5. Name any two chatbots where the machine interacts with you by your language.
6. Write any four examples/applications of Artificial Intelligence with their description.

Lab Activity

Create your own song

1. Go to the link: https://musiclab.chromeexperiments.com/Song-Maker/
2. The following page appears.

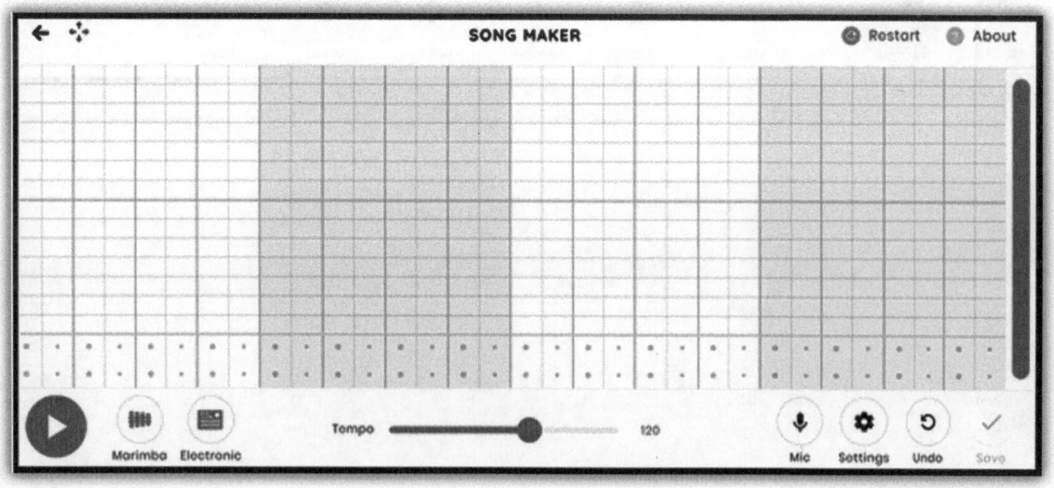

3. Click on the boxes to create nodes, and click on ▶ button.
4. The desired tune will be produced.

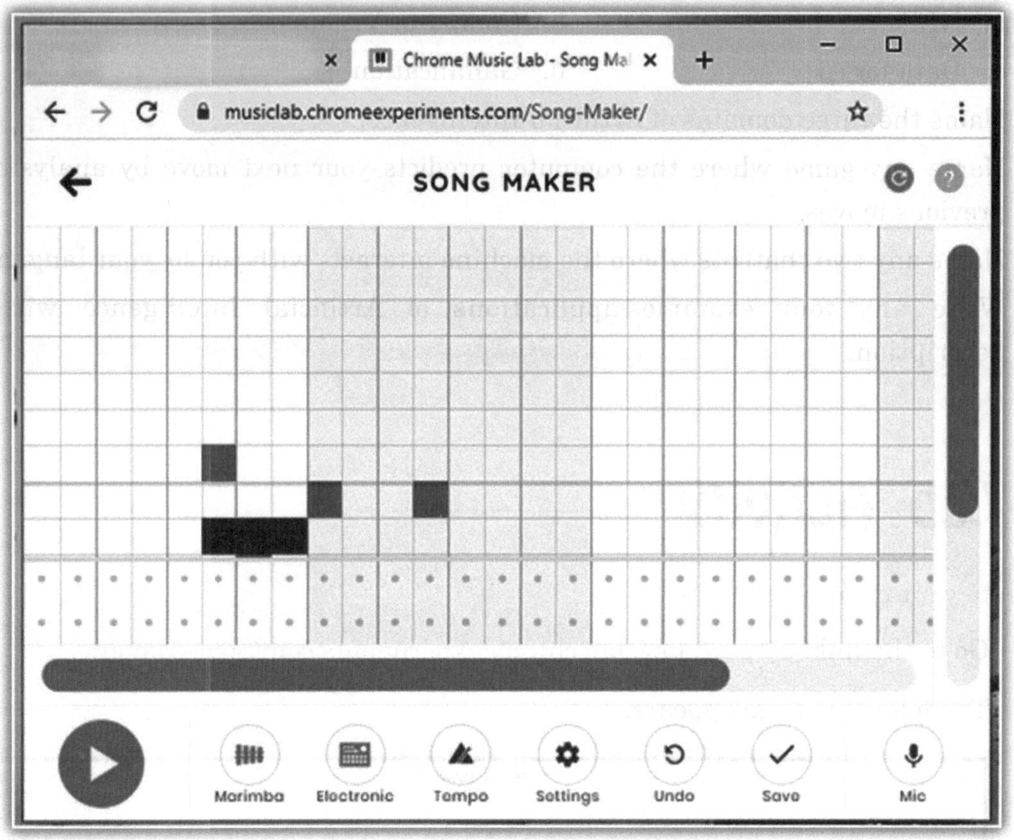

Worksheet

A. State whether the following statements are True or False.

1. Uber and OLA that matches one's ride request is decided by AI algorithm.
2. In video games, AI is not used.
3. AI system are based on logic and pattern-based algorithms.
4. Computer help users to find music and media of their choice on apps.
5. Robotics is the technology that is based on AI.
6. PUBG is a video game based on AI.
7. Emoji Scavenger Hunt is a web browser.
8. Rock-Paper-Scissors is a hand game.

B. Fill in the blanks.

1. There are multiple areas where _______has made a lot of progress in the past years.
2. ______________ is the process of adding game like components to a task so as to encourage under participation.
3. There are ______________pillars of AI.
4. _____________perform an action based on the command.
5. Smartphone gadgets are an example of ________________________.
6. ____________________like to collaborate, communicate, interact, and work in teams.
7. Object recognition and facial recognition are the latest development of ____________.

C. Write down the full form of the following.

1. AI ____
2. NPC ____
3. NLP ____
4. CV ____

D. Answer the following questions.

1. What is the main goal of AI?
2. What are the components of AI?
3. How is an AI used in games?
4. Write down any two uses of AI.
5. Explain the purpose of Smart Home.

QUIZ CARD

Multiple choice questions.

1. AI was first coined in ____________.
   - a. 1953 ☐ b. 1954 ☐
   - c. 1955 ☐ d. 1956 ☐
2. Another name of self-driving vehicle is:
   - a. Driverless ☐ b. Independent ☐
   - c. Dependent ☐ d. None of these ☐
3. With which technology the machine can see around and also collect information from images?
   - a. AI ☐ b. Chatbot ☐
   - c. NLP ☐ d. Computer Vision ☐
4. Who founded the Turing test?
   - a. John Turing ☐ b. Alan Turing ☐
   - c. Harish Turing ☐ d. None of these ☐
5. ____________is/are games developed by Google powered by AI.
   - a. Rock Paper Scissor ☐ b. Mystery Animal ☐
   - c. Scavenger Hunt ☐ d. All of these ☐
6. Banking, Smart Home gadgets etc. are the example of:
   - a. AI ☐ b. Chatbot ☐
   - c. NLP ☐ d. Computer Vision ☐
7. Which AI software can simulate a conversation with users in Natural Language Processing?
   - a. AI ☐ b. Chatbot ☐
   - c. NLP ☐ d. Computer Vision ☐
8. Which is used to adjust the house temperature?
   - a. Smart Home device ☐ c. Smartphone ☐
   - b. Smart Car ☐ d. All of these ☐
9. An estimated ____________Tesla cars are running in the US alone.
   - a. 40,000 ☐ c. 50,000 ☐
   - b. 60,000 ☐ d. 70,000 ☐

2 Relate with AI

Structure Bot

In this chapter, we will discuss the following topics:

- Web accessible resources to recognize the areas where Artificial Intelligence (AI) plays significant applicability in your daily lives
- Foresee one's expectations for future AI readiness and devise plans with the information amassed
- Create and play an interactive story using Google Story Speaker

Ideas Expectations

Objective Bot

At the end of this chapter, you should be able to:

- Demonstrate, discuss and elaborate how Artificial Intelligence can make your home, a Smart Home and your city, a Smart City
- Understand the use of Google add-on Story Speaker
- Interact and create an interactive story using Story Speaker add-on around an ultramodern home
- Evaluate the AI skills required for futuristic jobs

Dream Smart Home

Let us do a recap of your concepts learned from the previous chapter.

Activity 2.1

Share and write your ideas about Smart Home.

Figure 2.1: *Ideas and Expectations*

Label	Smart Home Gadgets
A	Smart Wall Projection
B	Projector
C	Smart Tablet
D	Smart Thermostat
E	Smart Workstation
F	Smart Bulbs
G	Smart Dustbin
H	Smart Dishwasher
I	Smart Refrigerator
J	Smart Water Purifier
K	Smart Treadmill
L	Smart Washing machine and Dryer
M	Smart Water Heater

Table 2.1: *List of Smart Home Gadgets*

FACT BOT

The Smart Home concept started with the invention of remote controls, unveiled by Nikola Tesla in 1898.

Activity 2.2

Revisit the Floor Plan that created earlier in Chapter 1. Identify and label the Smart Home gadgets in the given figure as per the following table 2.1.

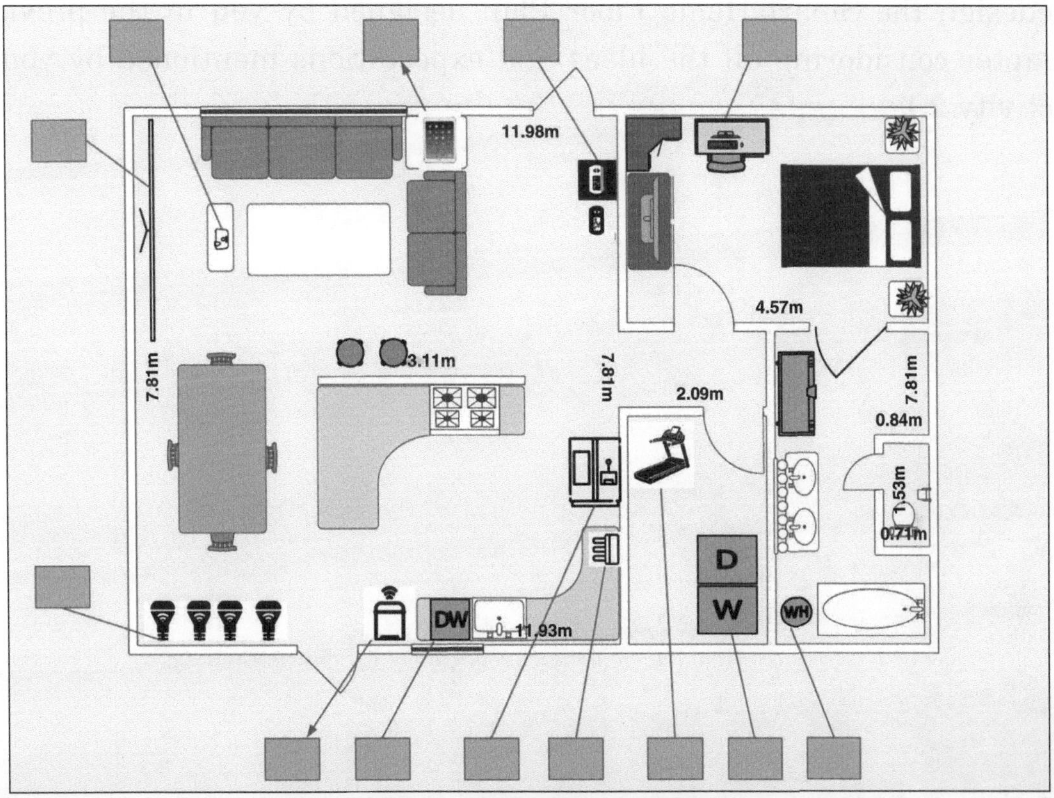

Figure 2.2: *Smart Home Floor Plan*

You shall watch the following video links to better understand the concept of a Smart City and a Smart Home.

- Smart cities video: https://youtu.be/bANfnYDTzxE
- Smart Home video: https://youtu.be/1CajaUoI3vU

Definition Bot

Smart City is an urban city which Internet of Things to collect data and information to improve the quality of government services easily and effectively.

Activity 2.3

Redesign the Smart Home Floor Plan designed by you in the previous chapter considering all the ideas and expectations mentioned by you in Activity 2.1.

Activity 2.4

List all the additions that you have done to your Smart Home Floor Plan.

1. ____________	2. ____________
3. ____________	4. ____________
5. ____________	6. ____________
7. ____________	8. ____________
9. ____________	10. ____________

Memory Bot

The main purpose of Smart Home device is to manage all of your home devices from one place.

Story Speaker

It is an add-on Google tool to utilize Google's voice recognition capabilities that lets you create talking, interactive stories without using and learning any coding language.

You can write a story in Google Docs, push a button, and play it instantly on your Google Home or any other device with the Google Assistant.

Prerequisite for Story Speaker

- Internet Service
- Google Account
- Install Story Speaker add-on to the Google account

If you want to share your story with more people, you can export it and create your own action on Google (this part is very experimental).

Steps to install Google Story Speaker as an add-on to your Google account

Step 1: Click on the following link: https://experiments.withgoogle.com/story-speaker

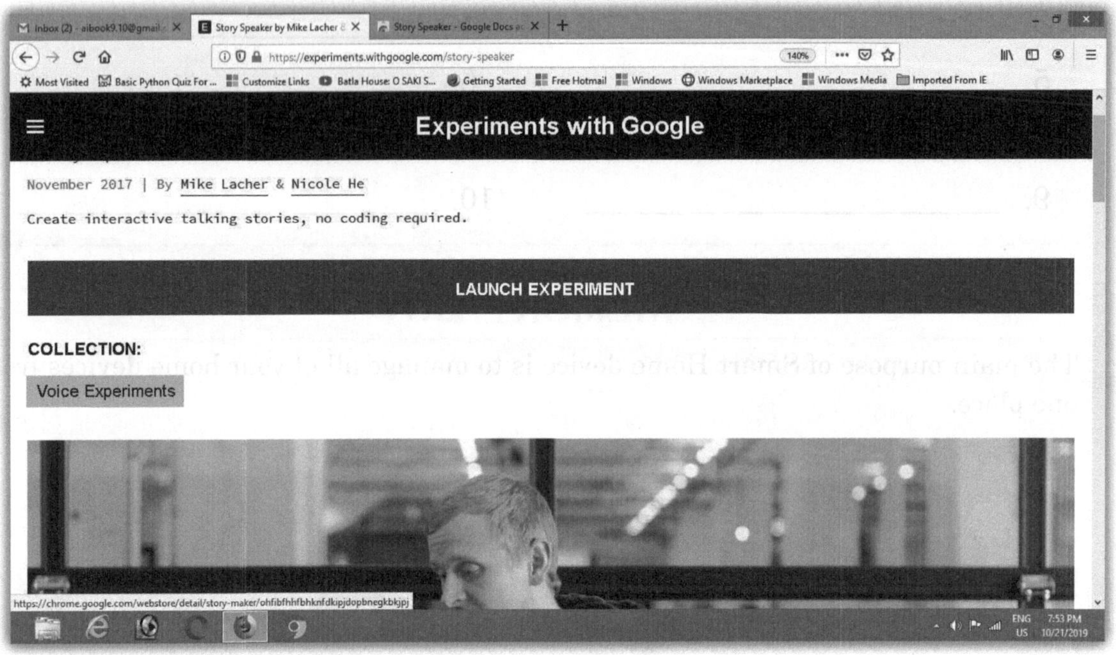

Figure 2.3: *Weblink image for adding Google Story Speaker*

Step 2: Click on Launch Experiment button, and you will be asked to give permission to execute the program.

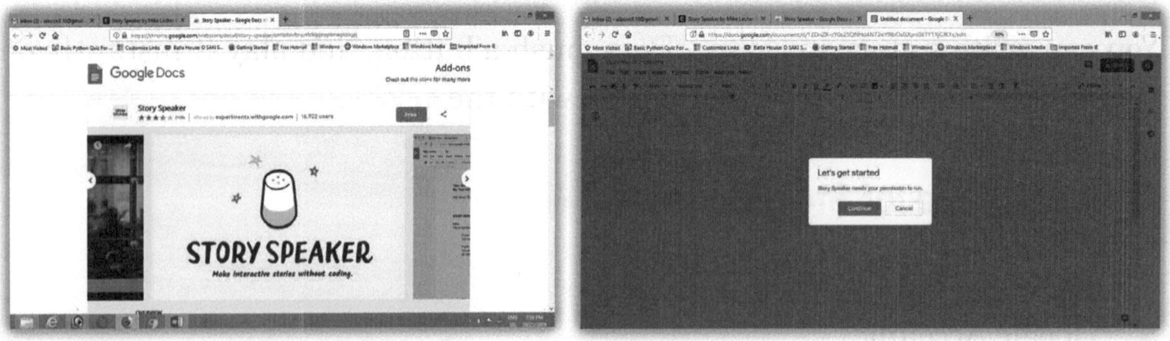

Figure 2.4: *Selecting the Google Story Speaker Add-on for your Google account*

Step 3: Click on Install button.

Step 4: Click on your account name to install the Story Speaker.

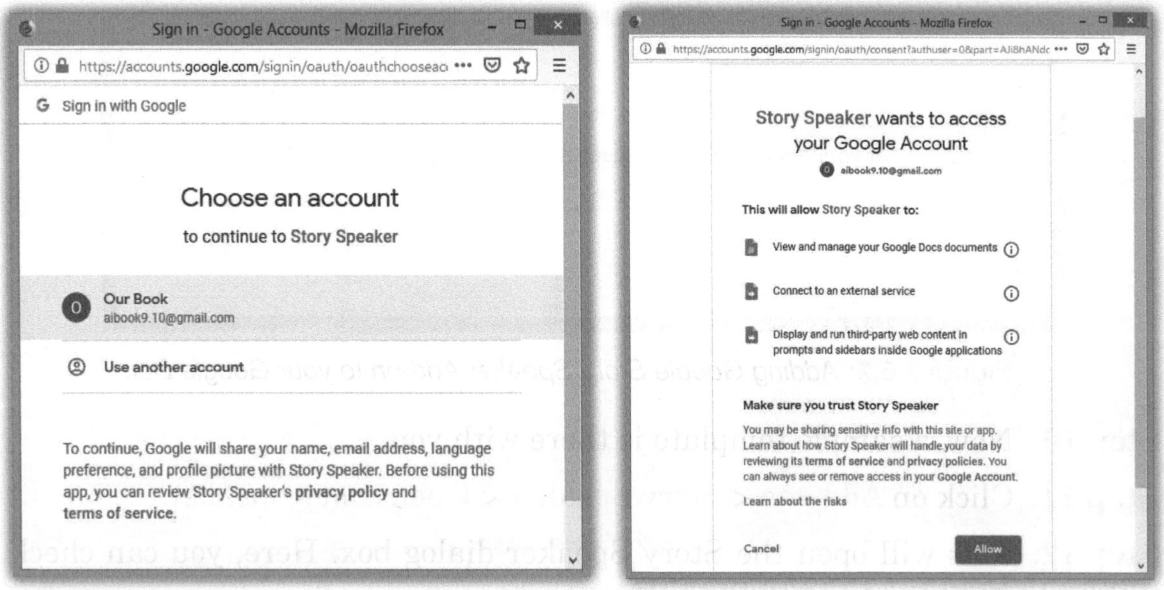

Figure 2.5: *Granting Permission to Google Story Speaker Add-on for your Google account*

Step 5: Click on Allow to give access of your Google Account to Story Speaker.

Step 6: This will open a blank Google doc named Untitled document.

Step 7: Click on Add-ons < Story Speaker < Create new story < From basic template.

Step 8: It will display a message to clear and replace your document with an empty template.

Step 9: Click on Yes and continue.

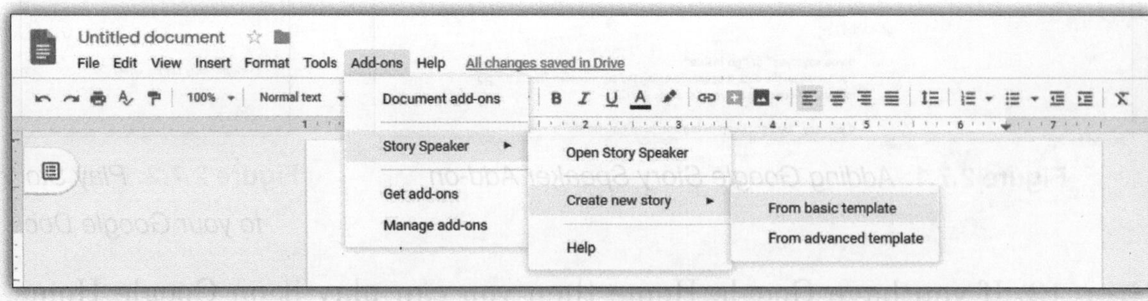

Figure 2.6.1: *Adding Google Story Speaker Add-on to your Google Doc*

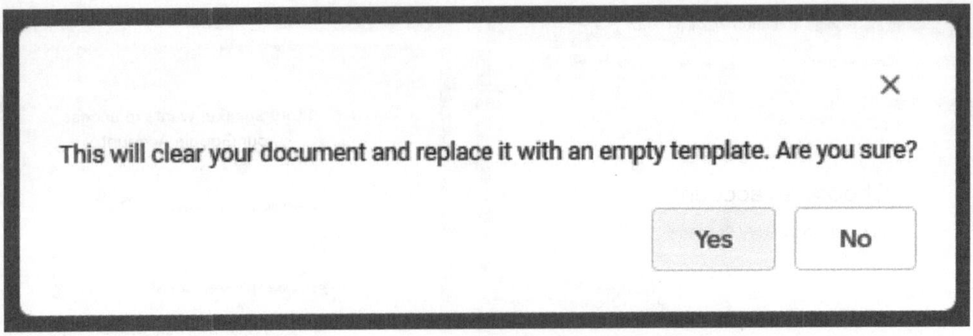

Figure 2.6.2: *Adding Google Story Speaker Add-on to your Google Doc*

Step 10: Now, a sample template is there with you.

Step 11: Click on Add-ons < Story Speaker < Open Story Speaker.

Step 12: This will open the Story Speaker dialog box. Here, you can check the story by clicking on the Play Your Story tab.

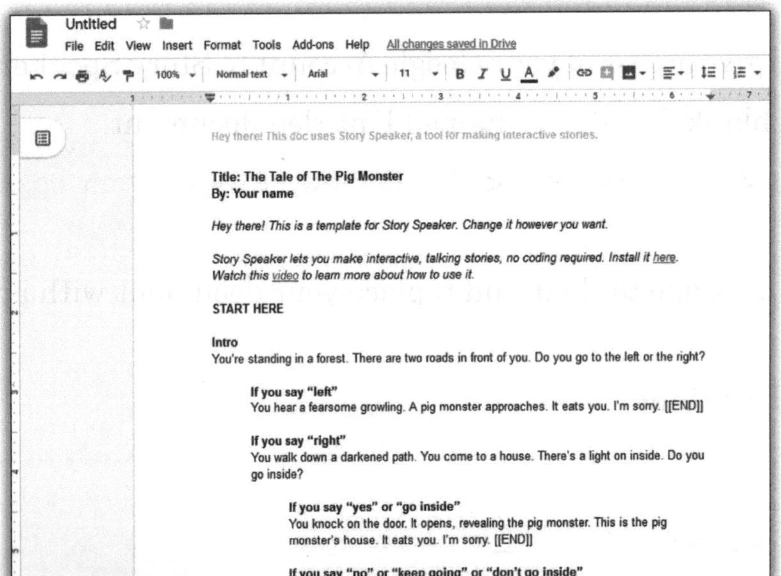

Figure 2.7.1: *Adding Google Story Speaker Add-on*

Figure 2.7.2: *Play Story to your Google Doc*

Step 13: If you have Google Home then you can play it on Google Home, or click on Play Story button below the Play your story in chat preview.

Step 14: This will give you the introduction of the story and then ask you to type in the choice asked. The moment you type from the options asked, it will reply as per the instructions from the story.

You can click on the Export tab to send the story to the Google Assistant and also anyone to play it. Remember to do the following:

- Keep checking your story while writing as it helps in writing error-free story.
- While writing your story, ensure that there is proper indentation for each of the text section.
- Add [[END]] to the statement where you wish to end the story.
- Also, ensure that you give proper specific instructions in the story that enables the story speaker to respond with an answer. For example, if you ask a question that you want to know the way to the bedroom, then the answer will be Walk a few steps straight, then take a left turn, and walk straight to the end.

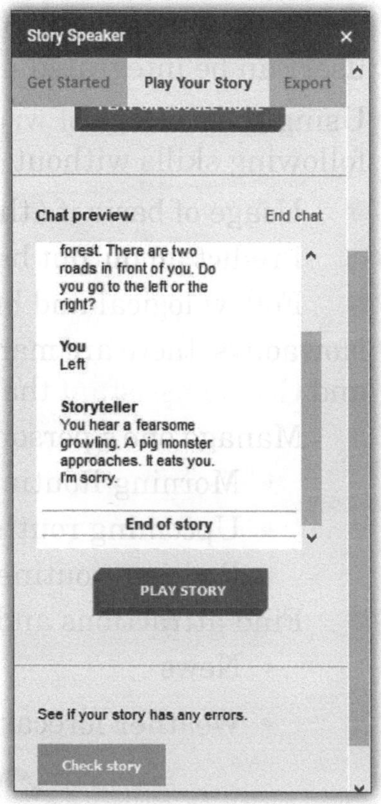

Figure 2.8: *Story speaker chat Window*

Story Speaker provides the templates, that is, a framework to write an interactive story. It has two templates the basic and advanced template. The basic template only has two options for every choice, and you can simply go and change what is provided there as what you want to say. The advanced template provides GOTO command. You can add random to make story look different each

> **KNOWLEDGE BOT**
>
> Story Speaker is an easy to install and easy to use tool and comes in handy when the user wants to create a story which changes according to the user's input.

time when you play it, and add saves so that the information taken from the user can be integrated into the story.

Using the concept of writing an interactive story, the students will learn the following skills without learning the coding language:

- Usage of basic if / then statements.
- Predict an output based on input criteria.
- Follow logical and branching concepts in a fun learning way.

Nowadays, there are many AI assistants available such as Alexa, Siri, Cortana, and Google Assistant that help us in a number of ways in your day-to-day lives.

- Manage one's personal list of daily tasks and routines:
    - Morning Routine
    - Upcoming routine of the day
    - Bedtime routine
- Find attractions and entertainment:
    - News
    - Weather forecasts and updates

Activity 2.5

By means of your Smart Home Floor Plan as a basis for your Google Speaker Story, use the Story Speaker extension in Google docs to write a story. Export and play your story.

TIP BOT

If you want to build a Smart Home, connect all your smart devices with both Google Assistant and Alexa.

The Story Speaker Add-on

The Google extension can be accessed with docs.google.com. After signing into your Google account, open Google docs. Go to Add-Ons option in the menu and choose Story Speaker. A dialog box will appear; choose Basic Template and work on the same.

Let us explore the basic elements and their flow that are required while writing an interactive story using Story Speaker. There are basic and advanced templates available which you can use and make certain changes as per your storyline.

The story has various elements with pre-defined purpose. There are certain lines in the story which are bold. There is a certain purpose of the bold statement, unbold statement, and indentation. The bold lines are not read to the user whereas unbolded lines will be read out to the user.

Let us discuss the various elements as per the flow from top to end of the story:

TITLE	This is the name of the file which is unique on your device and is required to play on that device.
AUTHOR	It is an optional attribute.
STAR HERE	A heading required before the start of the story.
INTRO	An introduction which will be played when the story is run.
PATHS	These are small sections with a bold line and unbold line. The bold line usually "If you say" is what the user will have to answer for, and the unbold statement followed by bold statement will be the output the user will get.
FORKS	This is when the user can make choice with the help of keywords after the: If you say "yes" or "yeah" or "yah" It's a bold line with a list of keywords on which you want something to happen. Write a statement below this in unbold so that can be performed.
FALLBACK	It is used when the user says something and is not matched with any of "If you say" and also, there is nothing defined that can handle it.
[[END]]	It ends the story. A story can have multiple ends.

Food for Thought

Activity 2.6

Let us put your thinking caps on and reflect on the activities conducted so far and fill the K-W-L-H Chart (Know-What-Learn-How Chart).

What we know	What we want to explore more	What we have learned	How we can learn more

Activity 2.7

Let us understand the importance of the following factors to be kept in mind while designing an interactive story using Google Story Speaker. You can tick (✓) in the appropriate scale box. (1-Least effective, 2-Somewhat effective, 3- Most effective).

Factors	Least effective	2-Somewhat effective	3-Most effective
Instructional words			
Clarity in thinking			
Order of events			
Language usage			

Activity 2.8

Based on your understanding of the concepts learned so far, reflect on the following.

1. How is the machine able to understand the instructions given by you?

____

____

____

____

____

____

2. What caused the responses to the questions asked by you?

____

____

____

____

____

____

TECH BOT

- **Smart Home:** It is the technology that uses-internet connected devices that can be controlled by your smartphone.
- **Smart City:** It is a city that incorporates Information and Communication technologies to improve the quality of living for its citizen through smart technology.
- **Story Speaker:** It is a tool that anyone can create interactive stories without any code.

Recap Bot

- A Smart Home is a home that can be managed remotely to control the items/ appliances/ gadgets/ systems such as TV, AC, fridge, and so on, with your device. All these devices need to be connected with internet. A Smart Home is actually a home with automation and thus called Home Automation.
- The dream of Home Automation wouldn't be possible without the use of Smartphones and internet connectivity.
- The IoT is used for building Smart Homes with automation and safety as priority for many of us.
- The Internet of Things (IoT) refers to all the objects/devices that have sensors, network connectivity, software, and so on, to connect in the network using internet and thus can make them responsive.
- Examples of IoT are security systems, electronic appliances, speakers, cars and many more.
- Smart City is an urban city which uses Internet of Things (IoT) to collect data and information so as to improve the quality of government services easily and effectively.
- The main goal of Smart City is to provide better quality of life to every individual.
- Story Speaker is an add-on Google tool which can help to create talking, interactive stories using Google's voice recognition without any knowledge of coding.
- The Story Speaker extension can be accessed using docs.google.com.
- The Story Speaker provides the templates for writing an interactive story.
- The two templates for story speaker are basic template and advanced template.
- Basic template of story speaker uses simple If statements.
- The advanced template provides GOTO command, add random to make the story look different each time you play it.
- The story can be run using Play Story in Story Speaker app or on Google Home.
- One can export the story for use in Dialogflow. From Dialogflow, one can publish it to the Google Assistant and share it with anyone.
- Google Home is a smart speaker which is a Google device and can be integrated with automation to control home appliances with voice recognition with the use of internet.

BRAIN BOT

A. Multiple choice questions.

1. A Smart Home is also known as:

   a. Home Automation b. Future Home
   c. Sci-fi Home d. Robot Home

2. A Smart Home is defined as:

   a. A mobile home
   b. A home which has enough food
   c. A home which is safe to live in
   d. A home that works on automation which is safe and secure

3. Which of the following devices can be used to control your security system remotely?

   a. Computer b. Tablet
   c. Smartphone d. All of the above

4. Can you use solar panels in conjunction with Smart Home products?

   a. Yes b. No
   c. Can't say d. None is mentioned

5. Are the Smart Home systems only geared towards a younger audience?

   a. Yes b. No
   c. Can't say d. None is mentioned

6. Which of the following can you do remotely with Smart Home technology?

   a. Turn on the geyser
   b. Check to see if you left the microwave on
   c. Turn on the shower
   d. All of the above

7. Is it possible for Smart Home technology to detect smoke and send a warning notification to your phone?

   a. Yes b. No
   c. Can't say d. None is mentioned

8. Story Speaker is an add-on tool by:

   a. Microsoft b. Apple

   c. Google d. Adobe

9. Use of Story Speaker is:

   a. Talking stories

   b. Interactive Stories

   c. Without using coding language

   d. All of the above

10. Which one of the following is an AI assistant?

   a. Car b. Robot

   c. Cortana d. None of the above

B. Fill in the blanks.

1. The dream of Home Automation is only possible with __________ and __________.
2. The __________ of Things is used to build Smart Home and Smart City.
3. The main goal of a Smart City is to provide better __________ of life to all.
4. __________ is an add-on Google tool to create interactive story.
5. Google Home takes __________ commands to work with.
6. Story Speaker provides the __________ to write an interactive story.

C. Match the following.

Column A	Column B
1. AI Assistants	i. Smart Speaker
2. Story Speaker	ii. Google E-mail
3. Smart Home	iii. Alexa and Cortana
4. Google Home	iv. IoT
5. Gmail	v. Google add-on

D. Answer the following questions.

1. Write any two best practices for building a Smart City.
2. Define Smart City in your own words.
3. What do you understand by IoT?
4. Write any two ways with which AI assistant can help in your day-to-day life.
5. Write any two examples of Internet of Things.
6. Define Story Speaker.
7. Write the prerequisites for Story Speaker.
8. Name the two templates provided with Story Speaker. Also, give one difference between them.

Lab Activity

To draw sketch of the picture online

1. Visit the link: https://photofunia.com/effects/sketch
2. The following screen appears.

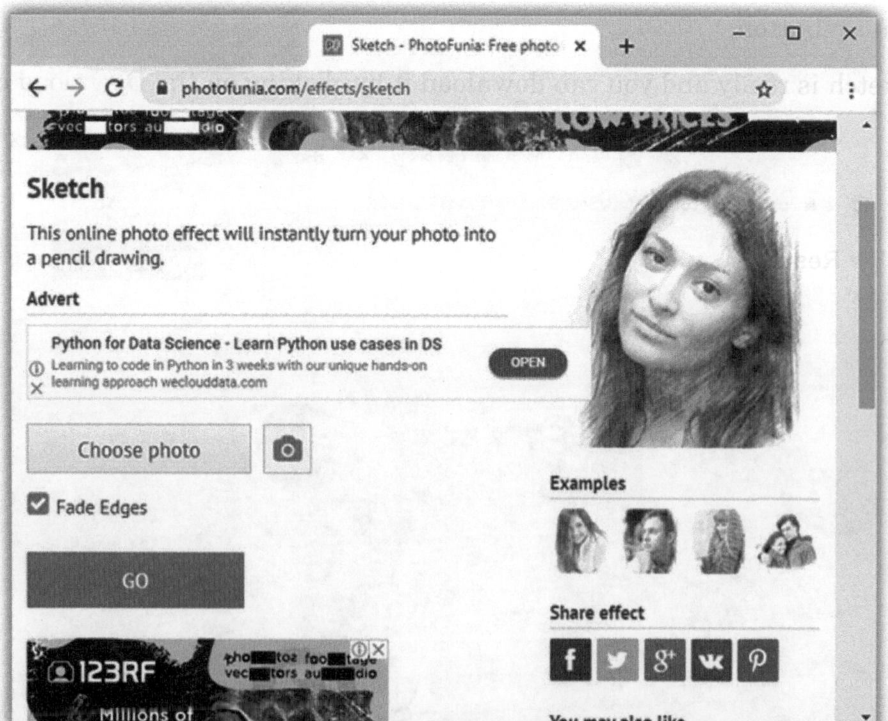

3. Click on Choose photo button.
4. Click on Upload from PC.

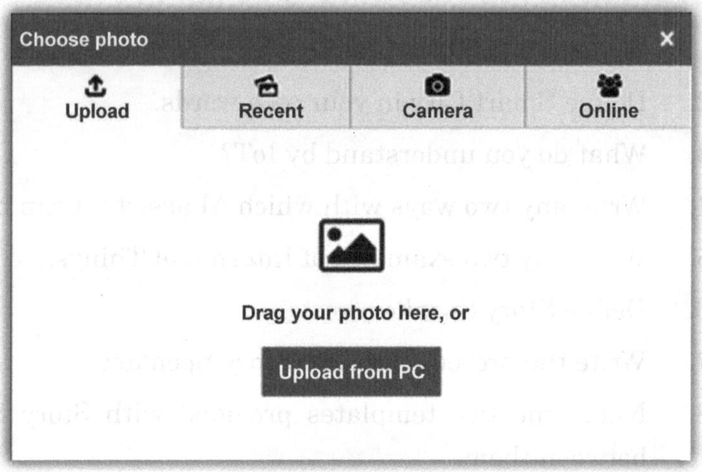

5. Once the picture is uploaded, you will get the following message to select an area of which you want to draw sketch.
6. Once the picture is uploaded and you select the portion of an image of which you want to draw sketch. You image will appear like this.

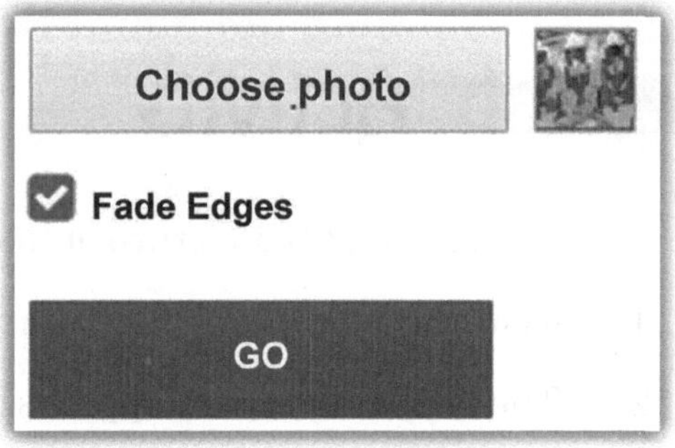

7. Click on Go button.
8. Your sketch is ready and you can download it by clicking on the Download option.

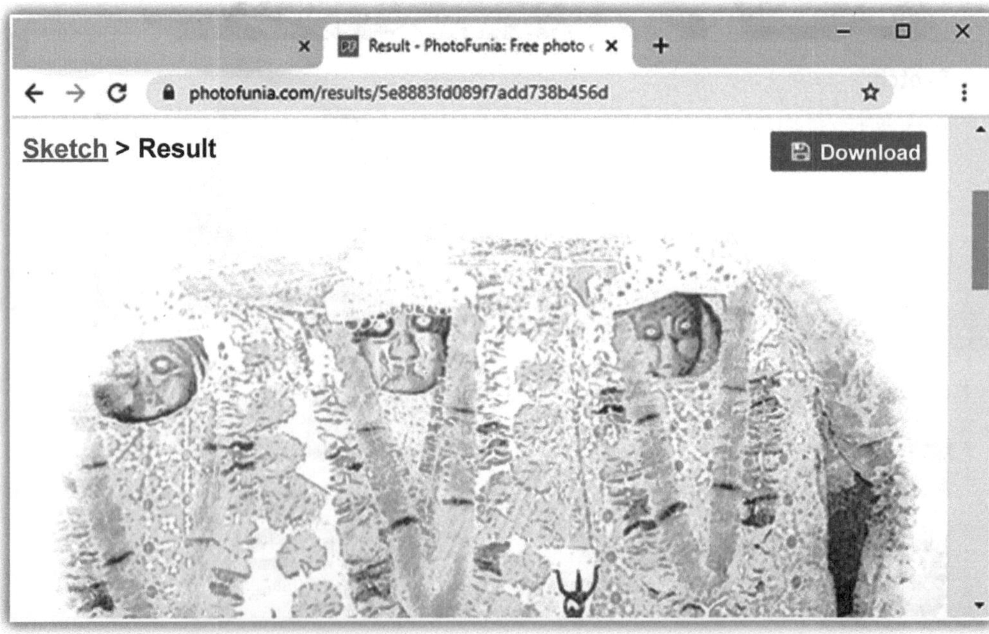

Worksheet

A. State whether the following statements are True or False.

1. Story Speaker has two template i.e basic and advanced.
2. The basic template provides GOTO command.
3. Cortana is one of the AI assistant.
4. The Google extension can be accessed with docs.google.com.
5. AI is an example of IoT.
6. Smart Home is also known as domestic home.
7. Advanced template of Story Speaker uses simple If statements.

B. Fill in the blanks.

1. The story can be run using Play Story in Story Speaker app or on ____________.
2. Smart Home devices need to be connected with ____________.
3. The ______________ is used for building Smart Homes with automation and safety as priority for many of us.
4. The full form of K-W-L-H Chart is ____________________________.
5. In __________________, the bold lines are not read to the user.
6. ____________________ help you in a number of ways in your day-to-day lives.
7. From ________________, one can publish it to the Google Assistant and share it with anyone.

C. Rearrange the jumbled words.

1. M G I L A ____________________________
2. A M S R T I Y C T ____________________________
3. O T I ____________________________
4. M P T E T E A P ____________________________

D. Answer the following questions.

1. What is the use of Smart Home?
2. Explain the use of advanced template in Story Speaker.
3. Define Smart City.
4. Write down the examples of AI assistance.

QUIZ CARD

Multiple choice questions.

1. Story Speaker is a:

   a. Google tool ☐ b. Microsoft tool ☐
   c. Mac tool ☐ d. None of these ☐

2. Advanced template provide __________ command.

   a. If ☐ b. If..else ☐
   c. GOTO ☐ d. Break ☐

3. __________________is a framework to write an interactive stories.

   a. Alexa ☐ b. AI Assistance ☐
   c. Cortana ☐ d. Story Speaker ☐

4. Home Automation wouldn't possible without the use of _________________.

   a. Smartphones ☐ b. Internet connectivity ☐
   c. Both a. and b. ☐ d. None of these ☐

5. _________________does not require any coding knowledge.

   a. Alexa ☐ b. AI Assistance ☐
   c. Cortana ☐ d. Story Speaker ☐

6. The story can be run using _____________ in Story Speaker app or on Google Home.

   a. Play Story ☐ b. Google store ☐
   c. Iphone store ☐ d. All of these ☐

7. From _______________, one can publish it to the Google Assistant and share it with anyone.

   a. Dialogflow ☐ b. Dialog box ☐
   c. Both a. and b. ☐ d. None of these ☐

8. The ____________refers to all the objects/devices that have sensors, network connectivity, software, and so on, to connect in the network using internet and thus can make them expensive.

   a. Smart City ☐ b. Smart Home ☐
   c. Story Speaker ☐ d. IoT ☐

3 Purpose with AI

Structure Bot

In this chapter, we will discuss the following topics:

- List and label multiple social issues ailing the world around us
- Understand the purpose of responsible citizenship
- List UN's Agenda 2030 of 17 Sustainable Development Goals
- Identify themes and social areas affected by local and global issues
- Gain an understanding of social issues through board game about Sustainable Development Goals

Objective Bot

At the end of this chapter, you should be able to:

- Demonstrate the need to become responsible global citizens
- Demonstrate, discuss,and elaborate various societal issues
- Identify purpose and relevance of 17 SDGs
- Understand, summarize and relate the societal issues where Artificial Intelligence can determine and solve the issues, locally and globally

Dream Smart Home

You have progressed from an agricultural to industrial to a digital age over the past 200 years. The motivation for a surge of industrial revolution has arisen from discovery and invention, hence defining new social dynamics. The scope of these innovations and advancement harbingers the transformation of an entire system of production of goods and services, political management, economic governance, societal structures, etc. that affects every sphere of human life. You need to put extreme efforts and measures to what is coming up in the next two or three years rather than focusing on what shall be the larger picture in the next decade.

As a responsible citizen, every member is expected to be an industrious, caring, conscientious and a contributing member of the society. Displaying empathy and compassion to one and all while being helpful and considerate towards one's society and environment reflects the good qualities of a good citizen. It is equally important to be a part of the change which affects the world around us.

Activity 3.1

Let us label every picture with the following social themes.

MEN OF QUALITY
RESPECT
WOMENS EQUALITY

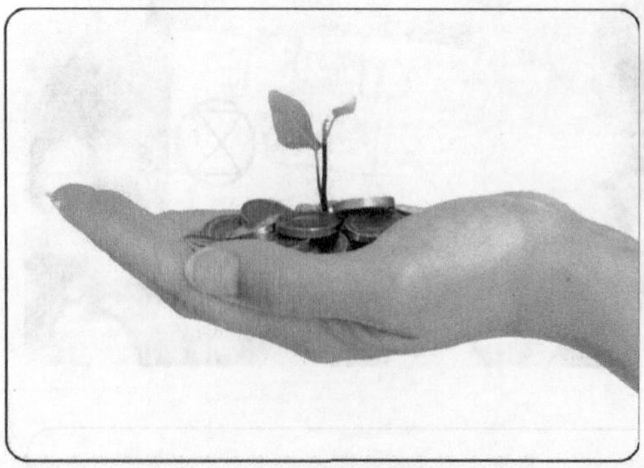

THE CLIMATE IS
CHANGING
SO SHOULD WE!
#ACTNOW

Social Themes

No Poverty	No Hunger	Good Health
Quality Education	Gender Equality	Clean Water and Sanitation
Affordable and Clean Energy	Decent Work and Economic Growth	Industry, Innovation and Infrastructure
Reduced Inequality	Sustainable Cities and Communities	Responsible Consumption and Production
Climate Action	Life Below Water	Life on Land
Peace and Justice	Partnerships to achieve the Goal	

Table 3.1: *Identifying Social Themes*

Definition Bot

The Sustainable Development Goals are the blueprint to achieve a better and more sustainable future for all.

Why should you learn about the Sustainable Development Goals?

The United Nations adopted the Sustainable Development Goals Agenda which includes 17 Sustainable Development Goals (SDGs) which came into effect from January 1, 2016. Many countries have committed to taking action to meet these goals which will aid in creating positive changes in local communities and achieving the SDGs globally by 2030.

Understanding about SDGs is vital for your learning. Some of the few reasons could be as follows:

- **You need to learn about the world:** You will grow up to be adults in an interconnected and multicultural society where you will need to be aware of cultural norms and differences around the world. The SDGs are global in nature and learning about these initiatives will help you develop insights into issues around the world which are undividable from culture, and to precisely understand the SDGs, you need to learn about the world around them.
- **You must be an active participant in the world you live in:** You have to be an active participant in your local and global communities to solve the world's biggest challenges. The SDGs will engage you in practical goals and problem solving by becoming a global citizen who is passionate about caring for others and society as a whole.
- **You learn about empathy and compassion:** You will begin to understand the unique challenges such as poverty, hunger and quality education, etc. communities face all over the world. You will be able to inculcate empathy and build compassion which makes you a passionate, engaged adult with healthy relationships.
- **You are inspired to take action:** Once you have an understanding of the SDGs and why they are necessary, you will be inspired to make positive changes in big and small ways.

FACT BOT

Fifteen years later, 193 countries adopted the 2030 Agenda.
SDG has 17 goals with 169 targets.

Activity 3.2

Let us observe the pictures and reflect your thoughts in the following graphic organizer.

Do you think you can make the world a better place or are you satisfied with the way things are around you?

Mention some points such as clean water, equality of gender, etc. where you can play a vital role for the well-being of your community and world.

Mention your thoughts that shall make the world a better place.

Mention your actions that shall make the world a better place.

Sustainable Development Goals

The directives which are outlined under the SDG umbrella can be collectively defined as the progress that meets the requirements of the present without negotiating the capability of future generations to meet their own needs. The goals signify rigorous efforts towards building a wide-ranging, sustainable and robust future for people and its planet. The goals can be collectively achieved when three most important essentials economic growth, social inclusion, and environmental protection are equally taken care of since they are necessary for the welfare of individuals and societies.

Certain requirements as exterminating poverty, unbiased economic growth, reducing inequalities, nurturing impartial social development and inclusion while encouraging cohesive and sustainable management of natural resources and ecosystems; our climate, land and water are important aspects to raise the standards of living.

KNOWLEDGE BOT

SDG objective was to produce a set of universal goals that meet the urgent environmental, political and economic challenges facing your world.

FUN TIME

1. What is the use of water in our life?
2. Write down the name of Goal 3.
2. What is the purpose of SDGs?

Activity 3.3

Let us look at the following video link to understand the SDGs better.

https://youtu.be/5G0ndS3uRdo

S.No.	SDG	Description
1	 **Image Credit:** By United Nations - UN.org/Sustainable Development, Public Domain, https://commons.wikimedia.org/w/index.php?curid=65335721	Poverty must be finished in all its forms everywhere; hence, implementing social protection system at national level.

S.No.	SDG	Description
2	 **Image Credit:** By United Nations - UN.org/SustainableDevelopment, Public Domain, https://commons.wikimedia.org/w/index.php?curid=65335693	Sustainable food production and agricultural approaches should be adopted universally to end hunger and malnutrition.
3	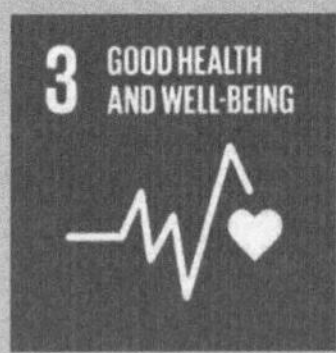 **Image Credit:** By United Nations - UN.org/SustainableDevelopment, Public Domain, https://commons.wikimedia.org/w/index.php?curid=65335671	The quality of the environment along with reducing number of deaths due to air, water, and soil pollution affect the good health and well-being of all.
4	 **Image Credit:** By United Nations - UN.org/SustainableDevelopment, Public Domain, https://commons.wikimedia.org/w/index.php?curid=65335655	All should have access to primary and secondary education with free access to vocational training while eliminating gender and wealth disparities.
5	 **Image Credit:** By United Nations - UN.org/SustainableDevelopment, Public Domain, https://commons.wikimedia.org/w/index.php?curid=65335642	Discrimination in all forms based on gender should be eradicated with equal rights to economic resources and ownership.

S.No.	SDG	Description
6	 **Image Credit:** By United Nations - UN.org/SustainableDevelopment, Public Domain, https://commons.wikimedia.org/w/index.php?curid=65335596	Health and wellness of all beings is a basic and critical goal with ease of access to clean water and sanitation facilities.
7	 **Image Credit:** By United Nations - UN.org/SustainableDevelopment, Public Domain, https://commons.wikimedia.org/w/index.php?curid=65335584	The aim is to correct the imbalance by ensuring that all have access to affordable, reliable and enhanced modern energy services.
8	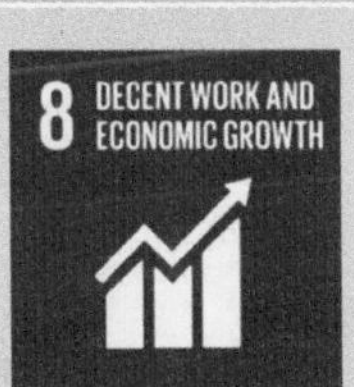 **Image Credit:** By United Nations - UN.org/SustainableDevelopment, Public Domain, https://commons.wikimedia.org/w/index.php?curid=65335570	Economic growth and higher levels of productivity with technological innovations will encourage job opportunities.
9	 **Image Credit:** By United Nations - UN.org/SustainableDevelopment, Public Domain, https://commons.wikimedia.org/w/index.php?curid=65335565	Investment in infrastructure and innovation are keys to finding lasting solutions to both economic and environmental challenges.

S.No.	SDG	Description
10	 **Image Credit:** By .United Nations - UN.org/SustainableDevelopment, Public Domain, https://commons.wikimedia.org/w/index.php?curid=65335496	The widening disparities need to be closed with effective policies to empower all regardless of sex, race, and ethnicity.
11	 **Image Credit:** By United Nations - UN.org/SustainableDevelopment, Public Domain, https://commons.wikimedia.org/w/index.php?curid=65335475	All human settlements, namely, cities and communities, must be safe, inclusive, resilient, and sustainable.
12	 **Image Credit:** By United Nations - UN.org/SustainableDevelopment, Public Domain, https://commons.wikimedia.org/w/index.php?curid=65335468	Many countries are moving towards encouraging industries, businesses, and consumers to recycle and reduce waste which is equally important.
13	 **Image Credit:** By United Nations - UN.org/SustainableDevelopment, Public Domain, https://commons.wikimedia.org/w/index.php?curid=65335462	It is imperative to take urgent actions to combat climate change and its impacts.

S.No.	SDG	Description
14	 **Image Credit:** By United Nations - UN.org/SustainableDevelopment, Public Domain, https://commons.wikimedia.org/w/index.php?curid=65335459	The world's oceans play an important part in human world. It is essential to conserve seas and marine resources for sustainable development.
15	 **Image Credit:** By United Nations - UN.org/SustainableDevelopment, Public Domain, https://commons.wikimedia.org/w/index.php?curid=65335452	The main impetus is to promote, protect, and restore use of terrestrial ecosystems, manage forests, and halt and reverse land degradation and biodiversity loss.
16	 **Image Credit:** By United Nations - UN.org/SustainableDevelopment, Public Domain, https://commons.wikimedia.org/w/index.php?curid=65335433	Promoting the rule of law and human rights, reducing all forms of violence, and to work with governments and communities to end conflict and insecurity are the main keys here.
17	 **Image Credit:** By United Nations - UN.org/SustainableDevelopment, Public Domain, https://commons.wikimedia.org/w/index.php?curid=65335420	Cultivating partnerships to share ideas and foster innovation to encourage growth and trade based on coordinating policies among countries is the key here.

Table 3.2: *Sustainable Development Goals*

Tip Bot

Solutions to global goals which include UNESCOs SDG Agenda 2030 requires effective planning.

Go Goals!

You know that games are an integral part of your lives. It becomes very easy to learn, understand anything in a play way manner. Now, as you have studied that there are 17 Sustainable Development Goals that you have to achieve by 2030 so as to make the world a better place to live for everyone.

Pre-requisites for the Game

To play this game, you need the following materials to start playing the game:

- Board Game
- Game Rule
- Dice and Token
- Question Sheets
- Scissors
- Colours
- Glue

Activity 3.4

Let us check your understanding by playing a game called 'Go Goals!'. To play the game, you must have the game as well as know how to play it.

Uses and purpose of each element of the game is given in the following table:

Board Game	It is similar to the snake and ladder board.
Game Rule	There are tokens for each player. One player will throw a dice and will keep moving on the board depending on the number that appears on the dice. The moment the ladder comes and the token will climb the ladder. If it is a waterslide, they move to the bottom of the slide. If the token reaches any of the SDGs, then the player is asked a question from the multiple choice question sheets. A correct choice from the MCQ will give a chance to throw the dice once again. The token which reaches first at 2030 is declared as the winner.
Dice and Token	The dice is used to play the game and move the token on the board. The token designates the player on the board.
Question Sheets	There are five sets of MCQs on each Sustainable Development Goals.

You need to follow the given steps and prepare your game which then can be played in groups in your class. Each member in the group can take responsibility of getting one element printed.

- Print the board game on A3 size sheet.
- Print the dice and then create a proper dice using scissors and glue.
- Print the player tokens and create the tokens using scissors and glue. Colour the tokens with different colours for each player.
- Print the multiple choice question sheets.
- This is not an online game.

Steps to get and create the game:

Step 1: Open the following website and click on Downloadable Material: https://go-goals.org/

Figure 3.1: *Screen of Go Golas!! Game*

Step 2: Click on Download Page option.

Step 3: Now, you can either register by giving the following details or else click on the cross (x) button and scroll down the screen. Click on Download.

Figure 3.2: *Register Page of Go Goals!! Game*

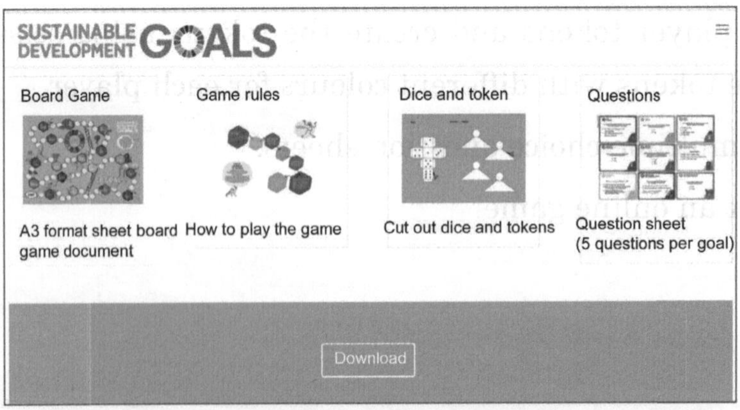

Figure 3.3: *Web representation of Go Goals!! Game*

Step 4: This will open the dialog Window to open or save the file in the designated path. Once you click on Open with/ Save File, click on OK.

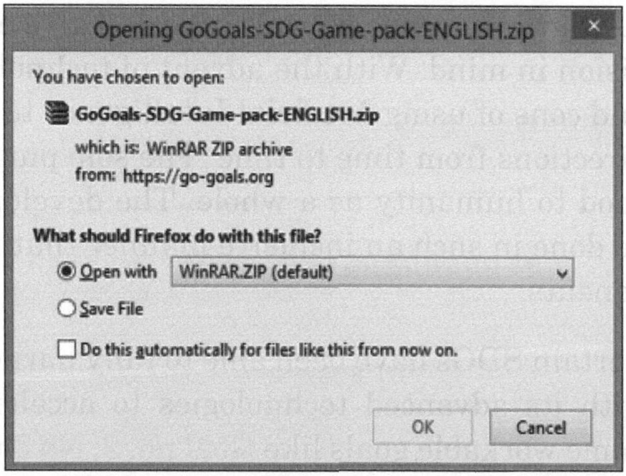

Figure 3.4: *Saving file in Go Goal! Game*

Step 5: Open the designated folder and then unzip the file. It will show you three pdf files as follows:

- **GoGoals_SDG_BoardGame_EN_web.pdf:** Board game to be printed.
- **GoGoals_SDG_Game Brochure_EN_web.pdf:** This will give you a review on Sustainable Development Goals, the SDG Go-Goals game, cutouts for dice and tokens, and rules to play.
- **GoGoals_SDG_Question_cards 1-5-EN_web.pdf:** This is used to create the five sets of multiple choice questions for each Sustainable Development Goal.

Role of Artificial Intelligence

Artificial Intelligence presents and magnifies your understanding to solve complex and interconnected global challenges such as hunger, climate change and life on land and water to name a few. AI processes augment scenarios such as computerizing routine tasks, analyzing big data, and generating intelligent solutions to a wide range of sustainable development issues. A well-designed AI solution can play a transformative role in helping us achieve the SDGs.

AI is growing exponentially and can give extraordinary results with a correct vision in mind. With the advent of technology, the scales concerning the pros and cons of using Artificial Intelligence to achieve SDGs have dipped in both directions from time to time. The sole purpose of AI usage should be to bring good to humanity as a whole. The development of such technologies should be done in such an inclusive manner that it is equally accessible by all for its benefits.

Certain SDGs have been able to fully harness the data-driven approach along with its advanced technologies to accelerate innovation at a global scale. Some workable goals like Goal no. 2, No Hunger; Goal no. 3, Good Health and well-being; and Goal no. 15, Life on Land; have proven results where AI has been constructive in providing solutions for the challenges faced. The crop yields are affected by pests which worsen with climatic changes. AI provided solutions where the disparities were checked and solutions provided to reduce crop loss and improve food production, thus resulting in No Hunger solutions for some communities. Certain AI enabled scans have been able to detect lung cancers better than regular CT scans, enabling good health and well-being. AI-enabled cameras have been developed which help forest rangers stop any poaching in wildlife locations with real-time data generated with human interference, providing solutions for Life on Land. The government's role in setting policies to help reap equal benefits of AI by all plays an equally important role.

Practice Time

Fill in the blanks.

1. SDGs is also known as________________.
2. The name of Goal 2 is ________________.

MEMORY BOT

The SDGs, also known as Global Goals, build on the success of the Millennium Development Goals (MDGs) and aim to go further to end all forms of poverty.

Food for thought

Activity 3.5

Let us take upon the role of a SDG commander. Identify a social theme problem in your community. Share your thoughts and plan of action that you would take to provide constructive solutions for the challenge faced.

TECH BOT

- **SDG:** It is a blueprint to achieve a better and the more sustainable future for all.
- **Go Goals:** It is an interesting game which enhance and check the understanding of the Sustainable Development Goals.

Recap Bot

- Each and every responsible citizen is expected to be an industrious, caring, conscientious, and a contributing member of the society.
- SDG stands for Sustainable Development Goals.
- Displaying compassion and empathy towards society and environment reflects the good qualities of a good and responsible citizen.
- The UN adopted the SDGs Agenda to achieve 17 goals by 2030.
- While learning about SDGs, you become an empathetic, active and a compassionate participant in the world you live in and get inspired to take actions.
- The three pillars of SDGs are economic, environmental, and social.
- Goal 1 aims to end poverty in all its forms from everywhere.
- Goal 2 seeks to end hunger and all forms of malnutrition and double agricultural productivity.
- Goal 3 aims to reduce the number of deaths and illness caused due to air, water, and soil pollution.
- Goal 4 aims to give free primary and secondary education while eliminating gender and wealth disparity.
- Goal 5 aims to eliminate all forms of discrimination on gender.
- Goal 6 is about health and wellness of all beings with ease of access to clean water and sanitation facilities.
- Goal 7 aims to correct the imbalance by ensuring that all have access to affordable, reliable, and enhanced modern energy services.
- Goal 8 encourages entrepreneurship and job creation with technological innovations.
- Goal 9 promotes sustainable industries, investment in scientific research, and innovation, which are all important ways to facilitate sustainable development.
- Goal 10 aims at reducing inequality within and among countries.
- Goal 11 ensures all human settlements are safe, inclusive, resilient, and sustainable.
- Goal 12 aims at moving towards encouraging industries, businesses, and consumers to recycle and reduce waste, which is equally important.
- Goal 13 aims to take urgent actions to combat climate change and its impacts.
- Goal 14 aims to conserve seas and marine resources for sustainable development.
- Goal 15 aims to promote, protect and restore use of terrestrial ecosystems, manage forests, and halt and reverse land degradation and biodiversity loss.
- Goal 16 aims to promote the rule of law and human rights, reducing all forms of violence, and to work with governments and communities to end conflict and insecurity.
- Goal 17 aims to encourage growth and trade on coordinating policies using improved technology and knowledge.
- Go Goals is an interesting game that can enhance and check the understanding of the Sustainable Development Goals.
- https://go-goals.org/ is a website from where materials for the game can be downloaded and prepared for playing.
- Artificial Intelligence can be used to solve complex and interconnected global challenges such as hunger, climate change, life on land and life below water, etc.
- Artificial Intelligence provided solutions where the disparities were checked, and solutions provided to reduce the crop loss and improve food production, thus resulting in No Hunger.

BRAIN BOT

A. Multiple choice questions.

1. SDG stands for:
   a. Supplier Documentation Group
   b. Sustainable Development Goals
   c. Strategy Decision Group
   d. Sustainable Design Group
2. How many SDGs are there?
   a. 19
   b. 12
   c. 7
   d. 17
3. What is the aim of Goal 1 which is about poverty?
   a. Reduce poverty to 90% by 2030
   b. End poverty in all its forms from everywhere
   c. Reduce poverty to 50% by 2030
   d. Help each nation to progress by reducing poverty
4. Which one from the following is not a part of SDG?
   a. Climate Action
   b. Gender Equality
   c. Provision of Internet to all
   d Clean Water and Sanitation
5. Which one of the following specifically talks about equality under SDGs?
   a. Goal 6: Clean Water and Sanitation, Goal 12: Responsible Consumption and Production
   b. Goal 4: Quality Education, Goal 5: Gender Equality and Goal 10: Reduced Inequalities
   c. Goal 2: Zero Hunger, Goal 7: Affordable and Clean Energy, Goal 8: Decent Work and Economic Growth and Goal 14: Life Below Water
   d. Goal 15: Life on Land and Goal 16: Peace, Justice and Strong Institutions
6. Which one of the following is not part of Goal 15: Life on Land?
   a. Promote, protect and restore use of terrestrial ecosystems
   b. Halt and reverse land degradation
   c. Halt and reverse biodiversity loss
   d. Halt the use of biotechnology and genetic engineering
7. Which one of the following is not applicable for Sustainable Development Goals?
   a. They are a legally binding international treaty that all nations are required to follow
   b. They encourage the promotion of health, well-being, and education for all, at all ages
   c. They explicitly promote innovation
   d. They include the development of sustainable cities, infrastructure, and industry

8. By when the Agenda of Sustainable Development Goals is to be achieved?
   a. 2020
   b. 2026
   c. 2030
   d. 2100
9. Sustainable Development Goals are designed to apply to which countries?
   a. Low- and middle-income countries
   b. Only countries where more than 50% of the population live below the poverty line
   c. Countries in Asia
   d. All the countries
10. Which one of the following is not a domain of SDG?
   a. Social
   b. Economic
   c. Environment
   d. None of the above

B. Fill in the blanks.

1. The ________________ adopted the SDG Agenda which includes____________ goals.
2. As a ____________ citizen, every member is expected to contribute towards achieving SDGs.
3. Many countries committed for taking actions to meet these SDGs by______________.
4. Displaying ____________ and ____________ to one another is a good quality of a good citizen.
5. The SDGs are global in nature and learning so as to develop __________and ____________ around the world.
6. In No Poverty Goal, poverty must be finished in all its forms from______________.
7. It is imperative to take urgent actions to combat ____________ change and its impacts in Goal 13: ____________.
8. The world's ____________ play an important part in human world.
9. Halt and reverse land ____________ and biodiversity ____________comes under life on ____________.
10. In life ____________, it is essential to conserve seas and marine resources for sustainable development.
11. Games are ____________ part of your lives.
12. Each and every game can only be played with a set of ____________.

C. Match the following columns.

Column A	Column B
1. SDG	i. Gender equality
2. The quality of the environment along with reducing number of deaths	ii. Decent work and economic growth
3. Discrimination in all forms based on gender	iii. Sustainable Development Goals
4. Go Goals!	iv. Sustainable cities and communities
5. All human settlements must be safe, inclusive, resilient, and sustainable	v. Good health and well-being
6. Economic growth and higher levels of productivity with technological innovations	vi. Game

D. Answer the following questions.

1. Name the three pillars of Sustainable Development Goals.
2. Unscramble the following letters to form a word.

   a. OASCLI b. USSENTLAAIB
3. Write any three reasons for learning about SDGs.
4. Write any two points of achievement in the following SDGs:

   a. Climate Action b. Reduced Inequalities
5. Write the materials for Go-Goals game.
6. What is the purpose of the following while playing the game 'Go Goals'?

   a. Board Game b. Token c. Question Sheets
7. Name the website to download the materials for Go-Goals Game.
8. State any two issues of gender inequality which you have observed from your daily life. Also, write suggestion(s) to attain the gender equality.
9. Write the name of the goal for the following.

   a. Goal 1 b. Goal 12 c. Goal 16

   d. Goal 8 e. Goal 3
10. Write an example of how Artificial Intelligence can help in achieving the following.

    a. Goal 1 b. Goal 7

Lab Activity

1. Go to the page: https://experiments.withgoogle.com/interplay-mode/view/

   Following screen appears.

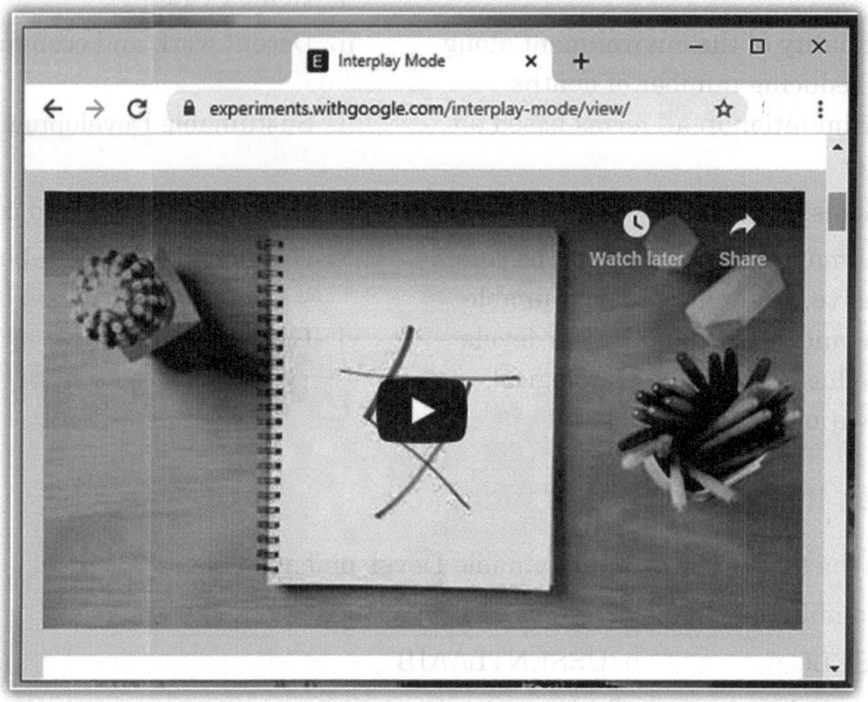

2. Scroll down the page and select Grammar lesson.

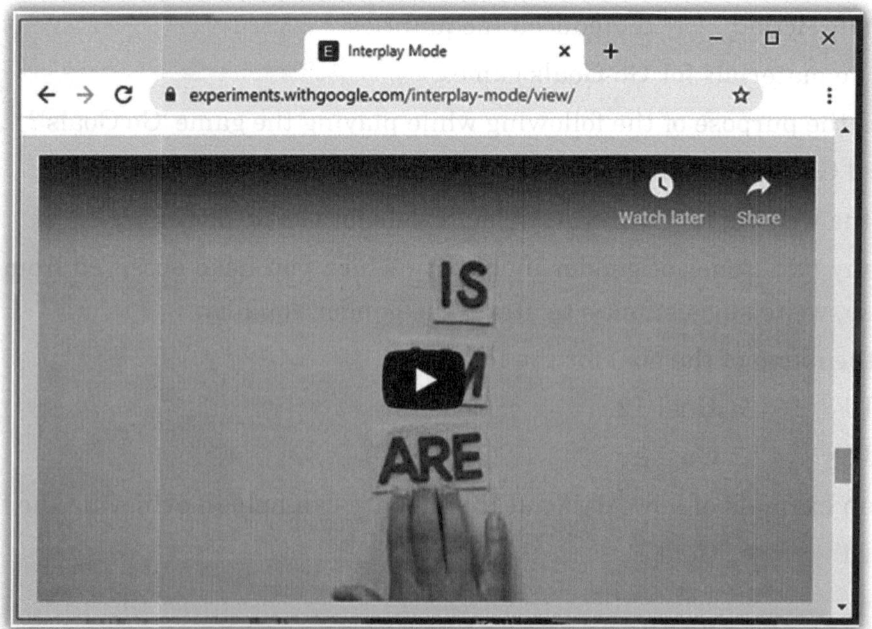

3. Play video, you will get to listen three different words.

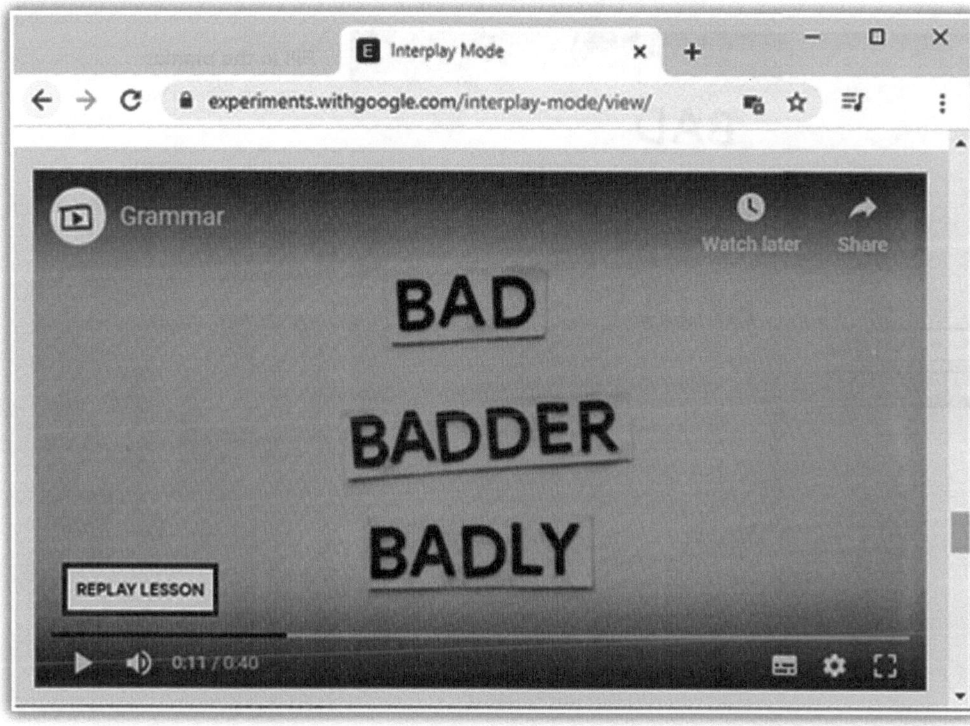

4. Speak the correct word and it will get display in the space given:

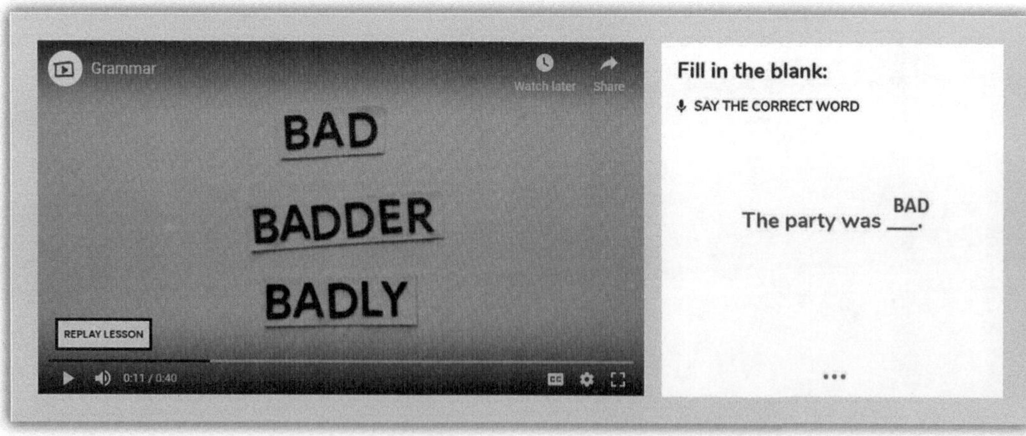

5. If you have spoken the correct word, the following screen appears:

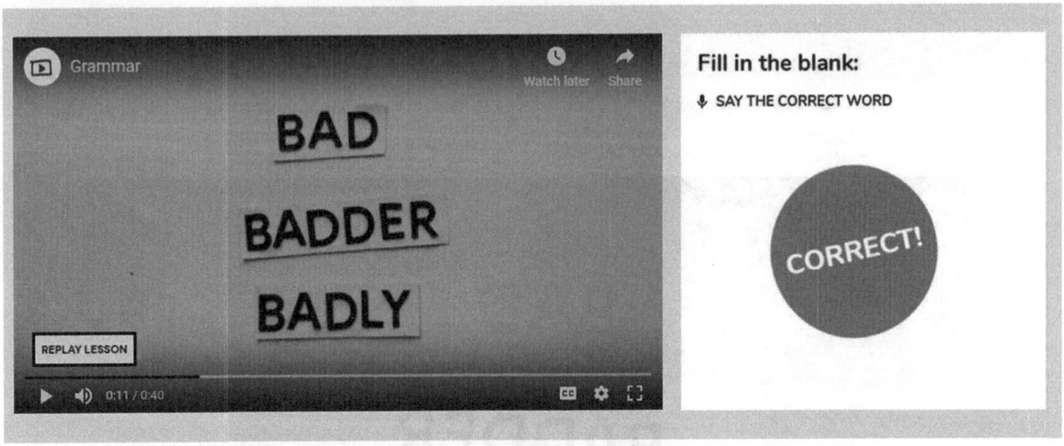

Worksheet

A. State whether the following statements are True or False.

1. No poverty means end poverty in all its forms from everywhere.
2. Go Goals!! can be used to solve only complex and interconnected challenges.
3. Goal 10 ensures all human settlements are safe, inclusive, resilient, and sustainable.
4. The sole purpose of AI usage should be to bring good to humanity as a whole.
5. Go Goals is an online game.

B. Fill in the blanks.

1. ______________ aims to provide education, at primary school level, for both boys and girls.
2. ________________ is to provide an affordable and reliable energy.
3. The SDGs are ______________ based and are interdependent.
4. SDGs are a part of UN Resolution________, the 2030 Agenda.
5. __________ aims to take urgent actions to combat climate change and its impacts.

C. Match the following columns.

Column A		Column B
1. Affordable and clean energy	i.	
2. Decent work and economic growth	ii.	
3. Industry, innovation, and infrastructure	iii.	
4. Reducing inequality	iv.	
5. Sustainable cities and communities	v.	

D. Answer the following questions.

1. What is SDG?
2. What is the purpose of Go Goal!! game?
3. Write the name of the goal 17.
4. What is the aim of goal 12?

QUIZ CARD

Multiple choice questions.

1. ________________ is a website from where materials for the game can be downloaded and prepared for playing.
   a. https://go-goals.org/ ☐ b. https://go-goals.com/ ☐
   c. Both a. and b. ☐ d. None of these ☐
2. ______________ aims to promote, protect and restore use of terrestrial ecosystems, manage forests, and halt and reverse land degradation and biodiversity loss.
   a. Goal 2 ☐ b. Goal 3 ☐
   c. Goal 12 ☐ d. Goal 15 ☐
3. ________ seeks to end hunger and all forms of malnutrition and double agricultural productivity.
   a. Goal 2 ☐ b. Goal 3 ☐
   c. Goal 12 ☐ d. Goal 15 ☐
4. The three pillars of SDGs are economic, environmental, and ______________.
   a. Social ☐ b. Socialist ☐
   c. Ecosystem ☐ d. None of these ☐
5. Sustainable Development Goals come on effect on__________year.
   a. 2014 ☐ b. 2015 ☐
   c. 2016 ☐ d. 2017 ☐
6. Goal 4 aim is to provide:
   a. Poverty ☐ b. Education ☐
   c. Hunger ☐ d. None of these ☐
7. Goal 5 aim is to provide:
   a. Poverty ☐ b. Education ☐
   c. Hunger ☐ d. Gender Discrimination ☐
8. ______________is used to create the five sets of multiple choice questions for each Sustainable Development Goal.
   a. Question Card ☐ b. Game Brochure ☐
   c. Board Game ☐ d. None of these ☐
9. The ___________are global in nature.
   a. Go Goal game ☐ b. SDGs ☐
   c. Both a. and b. ☐ d. None of these ☐

4 Possibilities with AI

Structure Bot

In this chapter, we will discuss the following topics:

- Explore the emergence of Artificial Intelligence (AI) enabled jobs in various fields and their impact on acquisition of skills required for these jobs
- Formulate a summary of findings of local examples of AI applications using the Research template
- List awareness points about AI bias and AI access along with the potential ethical concerns of AI
- Design a poster to summarize the skill sets required for AI-ready future jobs

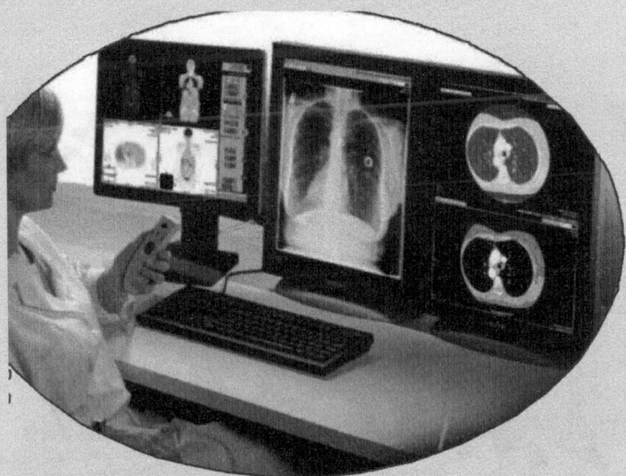

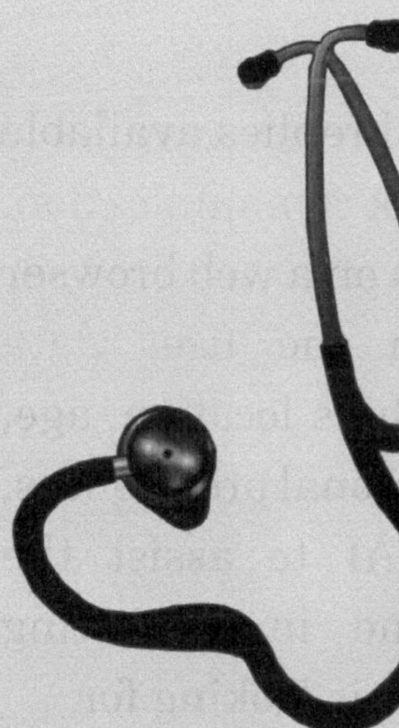

Objective Bot

At the end of this chapter, you should be able to:

- Describe how AI has been affecting jobs in various industries
- Paraphrase theme-based research of various local case studies
- Showcase and illustrate local case studies of people using AI for good or working in the AI field
- Identify and gain awareness on the skill sets needed for jobs in the AI field
- Home communication and collaborative skills while learning how to design activities

Artificial Intelligence plays a very active role in your daily lives ranging from:

- Checking your schedules.
- Looking for directions.
- Getting music and movie recommendations by digital assistants and chatbots on your hand-held devices.

Figure 4.1: *AI in your daily lives*

User preferences are deduced by data analysis done over time which are quite evident when exploring social media. The latest edition to this list is the successful launch of self-driving cars and parking assistance available in modern cars.

Smart E-mail replies available assist in quick communication. Smart search on a web browser is based on the user data collected such as location, age, and other personal preferences, which aids AI to assist the search engine in predicting what the user is looking for.

Figure 4.2: *Fiction vs reality*

Online purchases and travel bookings are other examples which are influenced with AI algorithms working in the background for user suggestions. The fictional stories of the past are now becoming a reality of your daily lives.

Definition Bot

Smart search is a simple interface that allows you to perform searches the way you would in a search engine.

Activity 4.1

Let us explore a few areas where Artificial Intelligence plays a major role. Mention a few examples observed by you in the following domains in the world around us.

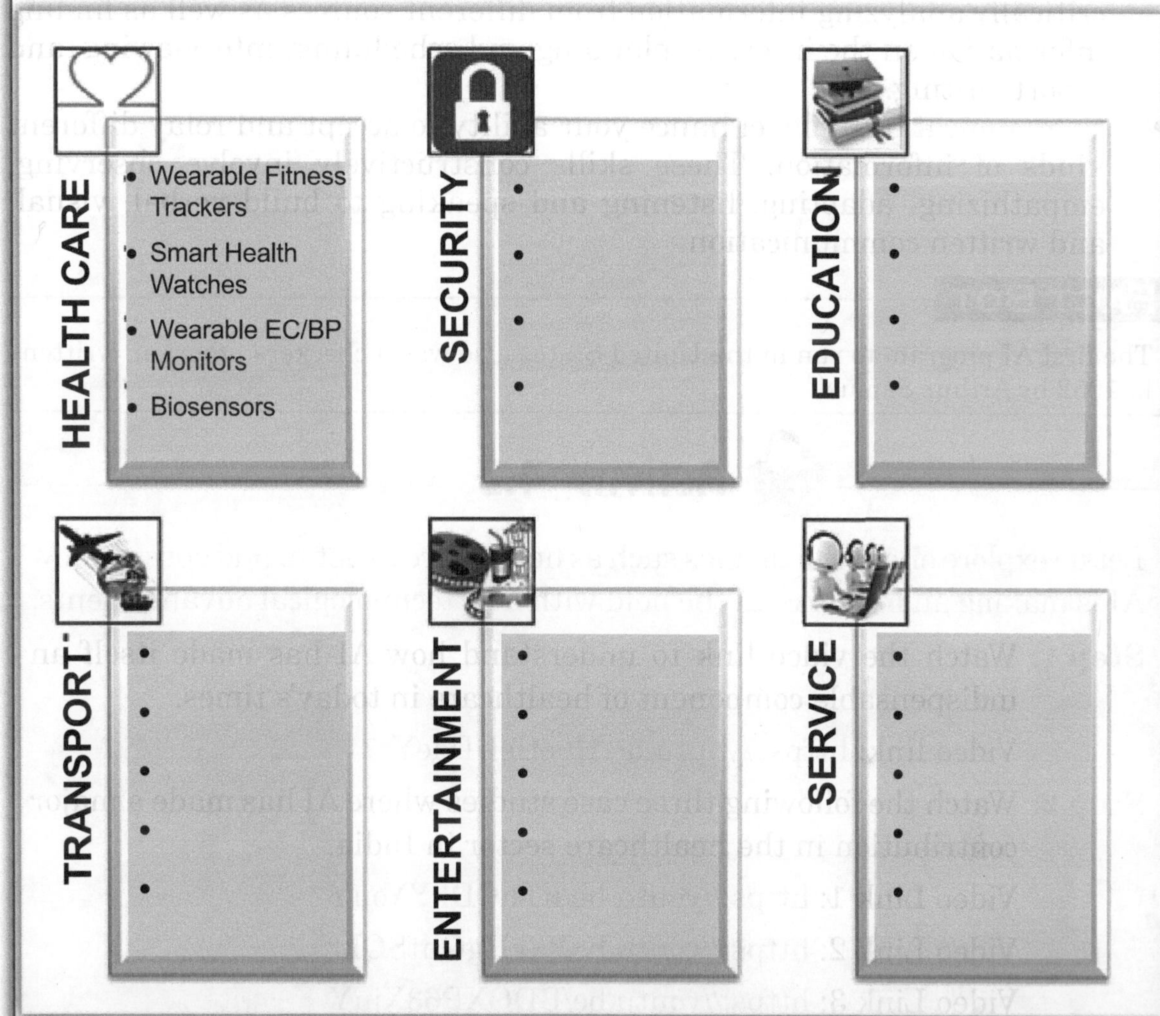

Figure 4.3: *Uses of AI in your daily lives*

Research Template

Before, you proceed towards understanding the themes more deeply, let us ponder over certain skill sets, research, and communication, which are crucial for understanding Artificial Intelligence in its true sense. You shall study and compose data using the research template explained later in the chapter to deduce your interpretations.

- Research skills attribute to suggesting new ideas and help comprehend the topic better. You can research using multiple methods like the internet, articles, studies, surveys, interviews, books, journals, experiments, and personal experiences. These skills further help you with data collection, critically analyzing information from different sources as well as finding information on the internet, planning and scheduling, interviewing, and report writing.
- Communication skills enhance your ability to accept and relay different kinds of information. These skills constructively involve observing, empathizing, adapting, listening and speaking to build verbal, visual, and written communication.

FACT BOT

The first AI program to run in the United States also was a checkers program, written in 1952 by Arthur Samuel.

Activity 4.2

Let us explore one of the themes such as healthcare in detail and observe how AI is making an influence in the field with new technological advancements.

Step 1: Watch the video link to understand how AI has made itself an indispensable component of healthcare in today's times.

Video link: https://youtu.be/H0etieBDxeY

Step 2: Watch the following three case studies where AI has made a major contribution in the healthcare sector in India.

Video Link 1: https://youtu.be/nTnCDkYYouY

Video Link 2: https://youtu.be/savHgQntSQk

Video Link 3: https://youtu.be/BDOXP63XjuY

Step 3: Make entries in the Research Template as follows to gather the observations post watching the videos mentioned above.

Industry Theme: Healthcare	
▪	AI is augmenting human beings and machines to work collaboratively to change the face of the healthcare industry.
▪	AI has permeated various areas of healthcare and probable futuristic applications to aid in saving human lives.

■	AI is an ever-growing hub of technologies that allow smart machines to broaden human capabilities and allow achieving more than they would have without the machines.
■	AI enabled smart machines can listen, understand, learn, and perform administrative and clinical healthcare systems.
■	Certain aspects of AI may create inhibitions among its users.
■	Healthcare AI is being implemented mainly in operational areas.
■	There is an improvement in analytical capabilities of the healthcare model in areas such as patient identification and personalized treatment and management.
■	The new systems are providing cost effective savings, (for example, appointments, financial treatment, and management).
■	There is an expanded patient reach serving broader population through digital tools.

Step 4: Mention the local start-ups or people working in the sectors using AI as per your theme.

What are the names of the organizations in your country working around this theme?	Write briefly what they do.
Zebra Medical Vision and Apollo Hospitals transform India's healthcare.	They are pioneering AI in medical imaging to enhance tools for radiologists to scan detect and mitigate to provide an all-in-one solution, including triage bone health oncology and cardiology. Apollo Hospitals are fully integrated with AI algorithms from Zebra-Med to help transform healthcare.
Google AI powered eye-care technologies at Aravind and Sankara eye Hospitals, Chennai, Tamil Nadu.	Google's AI has been using machine learning algorithms for diagnosing diabetic retinopathy. The same retinal scans are now being used for predicting the risks of having adverse cardiovascular events. They are bringing medical care to areas in interior India, where even the doctors are scarce.

Targeted Real-Time Early Warning Score (TREWS) developed by Machine Learning and Health Lab at Johns Hopkins University.	The concept has been using Machine learning to saving lives by going through a volume of patients' data and comparing them to one patient's health data to detect symptoms 12 to 24 hours sooner than a doctor could.
Narayana Health City	They have set up an in-house vertical data analytics centre using Microsoft AI for providing solutions from staff forecasting to enhancing prediction of diagnostic lab operations from volumes of patient datasets.
Qure.ai	They are exploring medical imaging space.
Sigtuple	Pathology.
CureSkin	Dermatology Solutions.
Niramai	Breast cancer detection.
Tricog Health	They have developed cloud-connected ECG devices which detect heart anomalies.

Step 5: Mention the skills sets required for the job sector as per your theme. Do elaborate on the set of skills (soft skills and technical skills) that would be expected of new hires, today, and after ten years.

Soft Skills	Technical Skills
• Work ethics • Interpersonal skills • Problem solving skills • Leadership skills • Interact harmoniously with other people • Communication	• Strong understanding of business administration and operations. • Basic understanding of medicine and patient care. • Financial software for planning and budgeting. • Data analysis. • Devising plans for maintaining Quality control standards online reviews.

Soft Skills (10 years later)	Technical Skills (10 years later)
• Communication • Team work • Work ethics • Adaptability/Flexibility • Interpersonal skills • Critical observation • Conflict resolution • Leadership skills • Problem solving	• Data analysis • Engineering and designers working with 3D printing • Research • Telemedicine • VR Technology experts • Machine Learning programmers • Using ICT to handle AI-enabled machines

Step 6: Mention the ethical concerns revolving around the theme.

Topic	Examples
• Cyber Security	• Added risk to patient privacy and confidentiality.
• Explaining the boundaries between the physician's and machine's role inpatient care	• User technical expertise in interpreting AI-guided diagnostic test results.
• Preparing future physicians for a career integrating AI	• Use of an Artificially intelligent robot during surgery.
• Legal issues	• Medical malpractice and product liability.

Step 7: Mention the sources and provide web links.

- https://www.hospitalhealth.com.au/content/technology/article/enabling-health-care-with-Artificial-Intelligence-423078316#axzz63fKkA71z

- https://www.hospitalhealth.com.au/content/technology/article/how-embracing-technology-can-make-life-easier-for-the-healthcare-sector-1163316087#axzz63fKkA71z
- https://www.webmd.com/a-to-z-guides/features/Artificial-Intelligence-helps-health-care#1
- https://www.pwc.com/gx/en/industries/healthcare/publications/ai-robotics-new-health/transforming-healthcare.html
- https://www.globenewswire.com/news-release/2019/10/28/1936480/0/en/care-ai-Collaborates-with-NVIDIA-to-Pioneer-Artificial-Intelligence-enabled-Autonomous-Patient-Monitoring-in-Healthcare.html
- https://www.healtheuropa.eu/personalised-cancer-treatment/87958/
- https://www.forbes.com/sites/greglicholai/2019/10/27/ai-policies-are-setting-stage-to-transform-healthcare-but-more-is-needed/#4c5b19d74817
- https://www.healthcarefinancenews.com/news/why-Artificial-Intelligence-wont-replace-doctors
- https://www.businessinsider.com/Artificial-Intelligence-healthcare?IR=T
- https://bmjleader.bmj.com/content/2/2/59.full
- https://bdtechtalks.com/2019/07/30/Artificial-Intelligence-health-care-trends/
- https://www.thebalancecareers.com/Artificial-Intelligence-is-changing-your-career-in-medicine-4586781
- https://factordaily.com/ai-for-healthcare-in-india/

The steps mentioned in the preceding practice activity can be one of the interpretations of the theme. However, you can summarize your observations as per your selected theme in the research template.

Knowledge Bot

- HDFC Bank has developed an AI-based chatbot called EVA (Electronic Virtual Assistant), built by Bengaluru-based Senseforth AI Research.
- Company like Microsoft are using AI to study land-use patterns with terrain maps.

Activity 4.3

This is a 4-pair activity. You can make a 4 student group pair and attempt this activity. Divide your roles accordingly. You have to delve deeper and fill the research template with your observations, keeping any of the following themes in mind.

Research Template

Industry Theme	
What are the names of the organizations in your country working around this theme?	Write briefly what they do.

Mention the skills sets required for the job sector as per your theme. Do elaborate on the set of skills (soft skills and technical skills) that would be expected of new hires, today, and after ten years.

Soft Skills	Technical Skills
Soft Skills (10 years later)	**Technical Skills (10 years later)**

Mention the ethical concerns revolving around the theme.

Topic	Example

Cite the sources and provide web links.

Poster making: Future Job Advertisement

A poster is a communication medium to present or promote an idea/theme to an audience. The focus is on the main idea and has to be presented in such a manner that it talks about the topic clearly by itself.

When you need to create a poster for future-ready AI jobs' advertisement, then it must have certain key elements in it. The key elements of the poster for such an advertisement are as follows:

- Title of the advertisement (Job designation)
- Short description about the company
- Number of vacancies and the post should be clearly mentioned
- Age and gender for the suitable post
- Location
- Remuneration
- Qualification: Educational, Technical and Professional experience
- Mode of communication
- Contact details

TIP BOT

AI help us to prevent future damage.

Activity 4.4

Let us continue with your theme healthcare as discussed in the previous section of this chapter and use the observations compiled in the research template. Now, let us design one advertisement for the same theme. Say, for example, I need to create the advertisement for an X-Ray Technician for my company ABC Hospitals.

To create a poster, first of all let us put the data in all elements as in the following table to make an effective job advertisement:

Title of the Advertisement includes the job designation	Radiographer, X-Ray Assistant
Short description about the company	ABC Hospitals has announced vacancy for X-Ray Technician urgently
Number of vacancies and the post should be clearly mentioned for which it is advertised	1
Gender for the suitable post	Male
Location, that is, the state in which it is required	Chennai
Salary	25,000 INR
Educational Qualification and experience (if any) needed for the post	Graduation with minimum 2 years of experience
Mode of applying (E-mail, postal, and so on)	E-mail: hr@abchospitals.co.in
Contact address and phone number for correspondence	ABC Hospitals, Chennai Contact: 1111111111

Once you have the values for the key elements, then you just need to put them in a presentable form in a box. Let us script the data mentioned in the tabular form to see how the above data can be presented in the form of a poster for job advertisement.

Required X-Ray Technician

ABC Hospitals has announced vacancy for X-Ray Technician urgently who is good at communication skills, medical, and anatomical skills and mechanical aptitude.

Total Posts	:	1
Gender	:	Male
Location	:	Chennai
Salary	:	25,000 INR
Educational Qualification and Experience	:	BS in Radiology program Minimum 2 years of work experience
E-mail your resume at	:	hr@abchospitals.co.in
Contact	:	ABC Hospitals, Chennai #1111111111

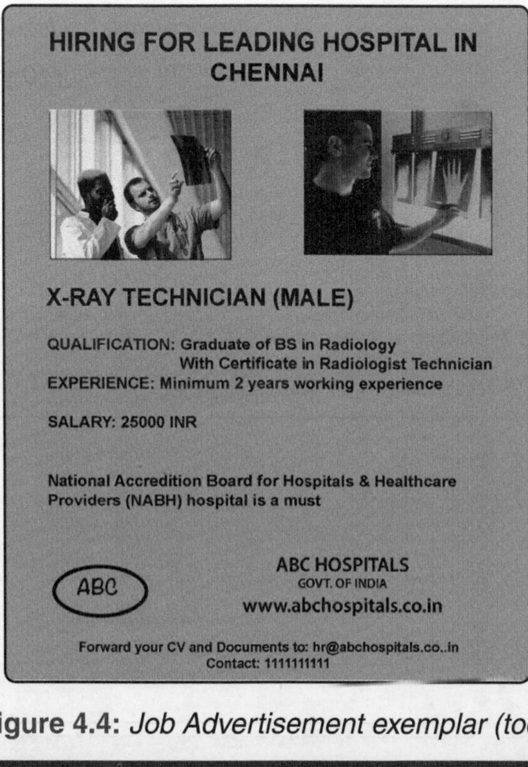

Figure 4.4: *Job Advertisement exemplar (today)*

Now as you have studied about the soft skills and technical skills that shall be required for the same job in the next 10 years, let us check out the soft skills and technical skills of the X-Ray technician which you need in your company.

Soft skills:

- Communication skills
- Team work
- Leadership skills
- Adaptability

Technical skills:

- Analytical
- Analyzing the equipment problems
- Calibrating and maintaining AI-enabled radiology equipment
- Medical and anatomical skills
- Data analysis
- Machine Learning

Figure 4.5: *Job Advertisement exemplar (10 years from today)*

Activity 4.5

Design a job advertisement for a professional from the theme selected by you depicting the skills required after 10 years from now. To create this advertisement, you need to search for current and emerging trends in this field and then create an effective advertisement.

Activity 4.6

Mention the soft skills and technical skills needed for the above advertisement.

Soft Skills	Technical Skills

MEMORY BOT

The best thing about AI in healthcare is that you don't even need to develop a new medication. Just by using an existing medication in the right way, you can also save lives.

TECH BOT

- **Artificial Intelligence:** It is the imitation or cloning of human intelligence, that allows machines, more specifically computer systems, to perform in an extremely intelligent manner.
- **Poster:** A poster is a large notice or picture that you stick on a wall or board, often in order to advertise something.

Recap Bot

- AI plays a very active role in your daily lives by digital assistants and chatbots on your hand-held devices.
- User preferences are deduced by data analysis which is done over time and that can be seen in social media.
- Smart search on web browser is also based on the user collected data by the AI assistance using data analysis.
- AI algorithms are working in the background all the time for suggesting online purchases and bookings.
- Healthcare, security, education, transport, and entertainment and service are the main domains/themes in which AI is playing a major role.
- Research is a skill which is used to get new ideas based and help comprehend the topic better. This can be done using various methods like newspapers, journals, internet, books, surveys, interviews, and so on.
- Research skill helps to collect data and critically analyze information from different sources.
- Communication skills enhance your ability to accept and relay different kinds of information.
- Communication skills involve observing, empathizing, adapting, listening and speaking to build verbal, visual, and written communication.
- AI is augmenting human beings and machines to work collaboratively to change the face of any kind of industry.
- AI is an ever-growing hub of technologies that allow smart machines to broaden human capabilities and to achieve more and accurate results in less time.
- AI enabled smart machines can listen, understand, learn, and perform administrative tasks.
- Soft skills are the attributes that are used to effectively interact with one another. Some of the soft skills are leadership skills, teamwork, communication skills, problem solving skills, interpersonal skills, and so on.
- Technical skills are the attributes and knowledge required to perform a particular task. Some of the technical skills are Project Management, Data Analysis, Designer, Writer, Financial Planning, and so on.
- Poster is a type of communication to present or promote something to an audience.

BRAIN BOT

A. Multiple choice questions.

1. Which of the following is not applicable for Smart e-mail replies?
   a. Save time
   b. Time consuming
   c. Quick communication
   d. Automated short email responses
2. Google AI powered eye-care technologies at Aravind and Sankara eye hospitals, Chennai, Tamil Nadu is working for/as:
   a. Dermatology solutions
   b. Breast cancer detection
   c. Pathology
   d. Diagnosing diabetic retinopathy
3. Sigtuple organization:
   a. Have developed cloud-connected ECG devices which detect heart anomalies
   b. Pathology
   c. Breast cancer detection
   d. Dermatology solutions
4. Which one of the following is not a soft skill?
   a. Work ethics
   b. Communication skills
   c. Data analysis
   d. Interpersonal skills
5. TREWS stand for:
   a. Training Range Electronic Welfare Simulators
   b. Targeted Real-Time Early Warning Score
   c. The Really Educated Work Systematically
   d. The Radio Electronic Welfare Simulator

B. Fill in the blanks.

1. User preferences are deduced by ______________ done over time and can be seen in social media.
2. Artificial Intelligence ______________ are working in the background for suggesting online purchases and ______________.
3. Smart search is a technique on web browser which is collecting user data by the AI assistance using ______________.

4. Research skill helps to collect ______________ and critically analyze information from different ______________.
5. ______________ skills enhance your ability to accept and relay different kinds of information.
6. Artificial enabled smart machines can ______________, understand, ______________ and perform administrative tasks.
7. Poster is a type of ______________ to present or promote something to an audience.
8. ______________ are exploring medical imaging space.
9. ______________ have developed cloud-connected ECG devices which detect heart anomalies.

C. Match the following columns.

Column A	Column B
1. Soft Skill	i. Data analysis
2. Smart Search on web	ii. Speaking
3. Technical Skill	iii. Chatbot
4. Communication Skill	iv. Project management
5. Digital assistant	v. Collect data and critically analyze from different sources
6. Niramai	vi. Dermatology solutions
7. Cure skin	vii. Teamwork
8. Research Skill	viii. Breast cancer detection

D. Answer the following questions.

1. Name any three themes for which Artificial Intelligence is playing a major role.
2. Unscramble the following letters to form a word.

   a. IKSLL

   b. ACEESHRR
3. Write any three soft skills and technical skills.
4. Give any two examples from your life where you have observed that AI is helping you.

5. Explain smart search on web with the help of an example.
6. Give any two examples of AI helping in the field of education.
7. Write the key elements needed to design a poster for job advertisement.
8. Write the functionality of the following organizations regarding AI:

   a. Google AI

   b. Narayana health city

Lab Activity

Draw your drawing automatically

1. Go to the link: https://experiments.withgoogle.com/autodraw

   The following screen appears:

2. Click on Launch Experiment button.

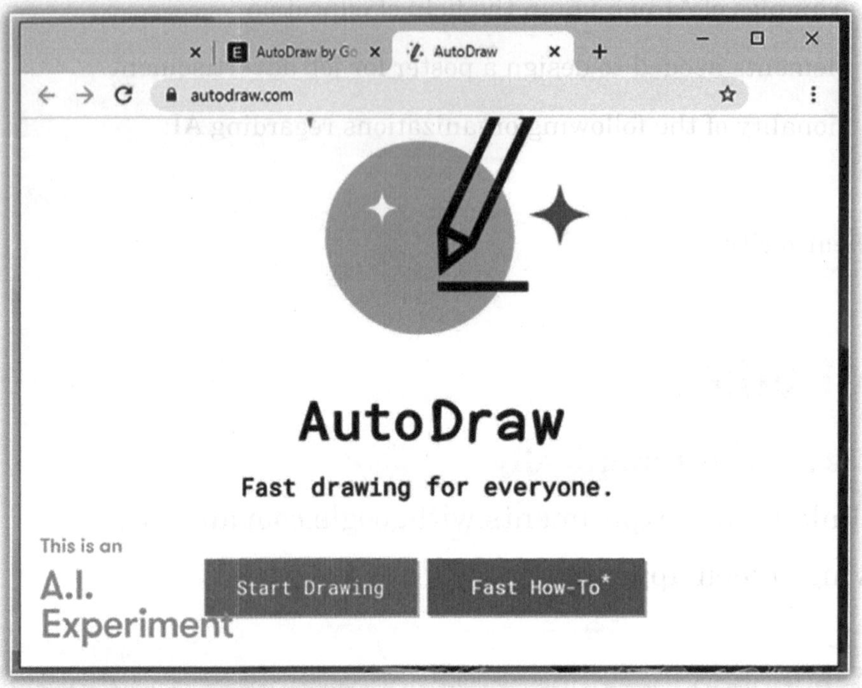

3. Click on Start Drawing button.

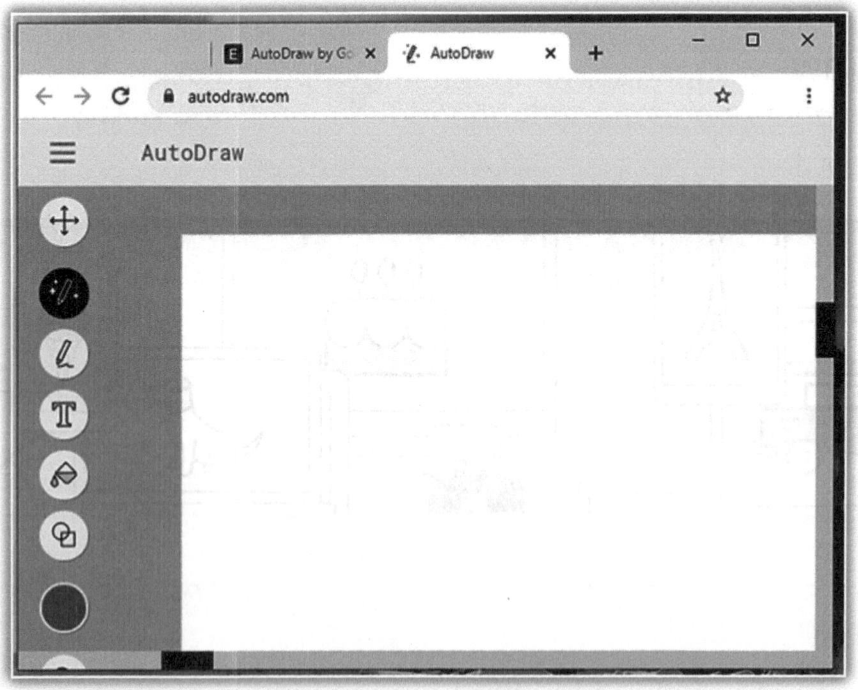

4. Select the AutoDraw tab.

5. Here, we draw a square.

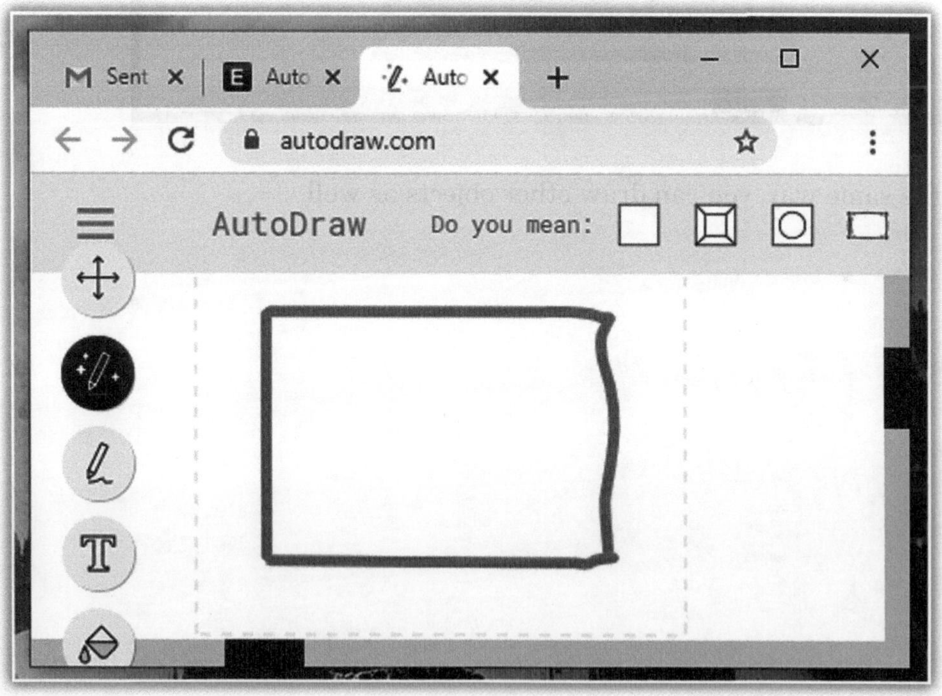

6. Once you stop drawing it, the suggestions of drawing will appear on the top.

From there you can select the drawing which you want to draw.

7. Here, we have selected the computer.The following drawing appears:

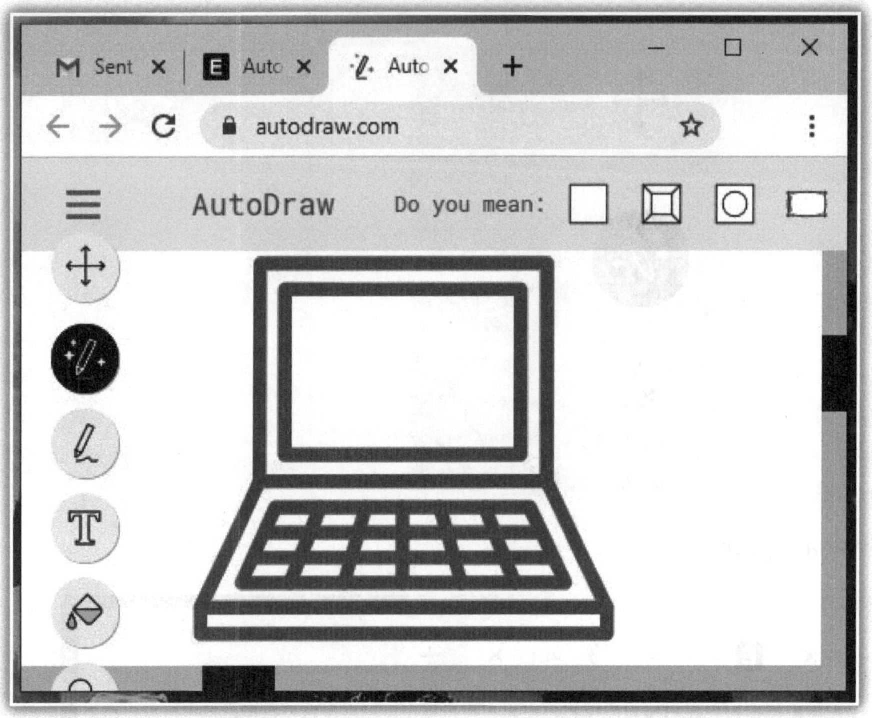

In the same way, you can draw other objects as well.

Worksheet

A. State whether the following statements are True or False.

1. Smart e-mail replies available assist in quick communication.
2. The fictional stories of the past are now becoming a reality of your daily lives.
3. Research skills enhance your ability to accept and relay different kinds of information.
4. You can communicate using multiple methods like the internet, articles, studies, surveys, interviews, books, journals, experiments, and personal experiences.
5. Google's AI has been using machine learning algorithms for diagnosing diabetic retinopathy.
6. Medical malpractice and product liability is an example of cyber security.
7. Title of the advertisement is a key element of poster making.
8. User preferences are deduced by data analysis which is done over time and that can be seen in social media.

B. Fill in the blanks.

1. ______________________ skills enhance your ability to accept and relay different kinds of information.
2. _________________ helps to collect data and critically analyze information from different sources.
3. ______ plays a very active role in your daily lives by digital assistants and chatbots on your hand-held devices.
4. AI algorithms are working in the background all the time for suggesting ___________ and bookings.
5. ________is a skill which is used to get new ideas based and help comprehend the topic better.
6. _______________skills are the attributes and knowledge required to perform a particular task.
7. __________skills are the attributes that are used to effectively interact with one another.

C. Answer the following questions.

1. Define Poster.
2. Explain communication skills.
3. Explain Google Smart.

QUIZ CARD

Multiple choice questions.

1. Which bank has developed an AI-based chatbot called EVA?
   a. ICICI ☐ b. State Bank of India ☐
   c. HDFC ☐ d. PNB ☐
2. The first AI program to run in the ________________.
   a. United State ☐ b. China ☐
   c. Russia ☐ d. Japan ☐
3. AI help us to prevent ________________ damage.
   a. Past ☐ b. Present ☐
   c. Future ☐ d. None of these ☐
4. Which allows you to perform searches the way you would in a search engine?
   a. Smart e-mail ☐ b. Smart Search ☐
   c. Both a. and b. ☐ d. None of these ☐
5. Company like ________________are using AI to study land-use patterns with terrain maps.
   a. Apple ☐ b. Wipro ☐
   c. Infosys ☐ d. Microsoft ☐
6. ________________is/are soft skills.
   a. Leadership skills ☐ b. Teamwork ☐
   c. Communication skills ☐ d. All of these ☐
7. Interpersonal skills is an example of:
   a. Technical skills ☐ b. Soft skills ☐
   c. Both a. and b. ☐ d. None of these ☐
8. AI is an ever-growing hub of technologies that allow ____________ to broaden human capabilities and to achieve more and accurate results in less time.
   a. Smart Machine ☐ b. Smart E-mail ☐
   c. Smart Search ☐ d. Both a. and b. ☐

5 AI Ethics

Structure Bot

In this chapter, we will discuss the following topics:

- Introduce the learner about ethical issues around Artificial Intelligence (AI)
- Deliberate and discuss about the complexities of concepts surrounding ethics (bias, access, privacy) in AI
- List awareness points about AI bias and AI access along with the potential ethical concerns of AI
- Debate around the pros and cons of ethical issues around AI
- Reflect and paraphrase how the emerging trends in different fields are getting affected by AI

Objective Bot

At the end of this chapter, you should be able to:

- Understand and reflect on ethical issues around AI
- Gain awareness around AI bias and AI access
- Compare and contrast the societal advantages and disadvantages of AI inclusion
- Recapitulate and reflect about the implications of AI

In the previous chapters, you learned to identify and appreciate Artificial Intelligence and describe its applications in your daily lives. You went ahead and performed activities to relate, apply, and reflect on the Human-Machine Interactions. You also made in roads in understanding the impact of Artificial Intelligence on Sustainable Development Goals to develop responsible citizenship skills as a global citizen. It was crucial for us to imagine, examine, and reflect on the skills required for futuristic job opportunities and understand whether you have the desired skill sets for such jobs. In this chapter, let us gain awareness about the ethical issues surrounding AI and comprehend its societal impact.

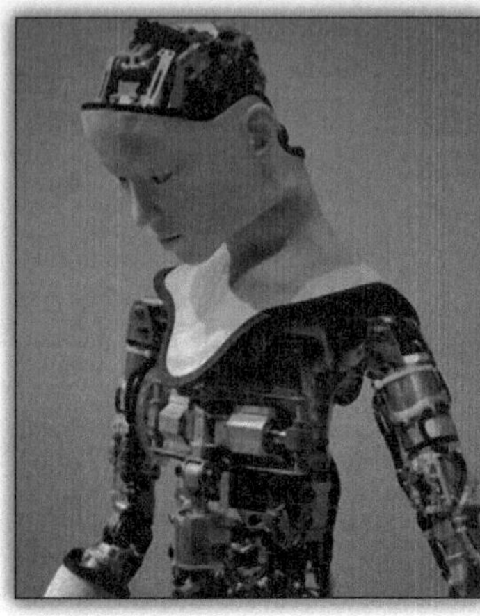

Figure 5.1: *A robot*

Activity 5.1

Activity 5.1: Let us watch the video in the given link and pen down your observations in the graphic organizer.

Video Link: https://youtu.be/vgUWKXVvO9Q

What have you understood from the video?

Mention a few learnings from the video.

What could be the theme heading of the discussion in the video?

What is the meaning of the content shared in the video?

Image credit: *http://www.smbc-comics.com/index.php?db=comic$id=1879*

Figure 5.2: *A possible conversation from future*

AI Ethics

Ethics can be broadly defined as the study of values; generating moral values for good and bad, right and wrong. Ethics plays a major role in many scientific researches such as stem cell research, cloning/genetically modified food, nuclear technology, animal rights, medical trials, disease research, and bio-warfare. New technologies have unintended negative side effects. Scientists and engineers must find ways on how to handle future projects. Certain myths prevalent around the concept of AI ethics are as follows:

- People might lose their jobs to automation.
- People might have too much (or too little) leisure time.
- People might lose their sense of being unique.
- People might lose some of their privacy rights.
- The use of AI systems might result in a loss of accountability.
- The success of AI might mean the end of the human race.

Figure 5.3: *AI in action*

Definition Bot

The discipline dealing with right vs wrong, and the moral obligations and duties of humans. It called AI ethics.

Artificial Intelligence is a form of technique by means of which computers can perform cognitive tasks that could be done by only humans earlier. Working on data, making sense of data up to a point where they could help us make decisions. There are many approaches among AI. One of them is where AI focuses on data-based AI and algorithms could be written to work with AI and further interpret this data. Another approach could be knowledge and context where data could be placed in different categories. Knowledge-based approach works best for expert systems whereas data-based AI is best matched with pattern recognition, image recognition, and speech recognition.

AI bias; also referred as Machine Learning bias, is a phenomenon that occurs when an algorithm produces discriminatory results due to flawed assumptions. There could be built-in biases created by programmers who have certain preferences. These go unnoticed until the algorithms are used and magnified visibly.

Figure 5.4: *How AI helps to solve problems*

We believe that these intelligent systems are supposed to make your life easier, but they are prone to amplify sexist and racist biases from the real world. Certain biases such as people belonging to a community are responsible for most crimes, gender requirement for some high-profile jobs or misinterpretation of social media posts due to wrong language translation by the algorithms used are just to name a few.

AI is used to expand abilities of people so that they can delve into creative spaces and accomplish more in their lives.

AI access can be defined as the mission where world's information can be organized and made universally accessible and useful to all. AI inclusion suggests making researches, tools, systems and scientific developments

FACT BOT

AI Access Foundation is a non-profit public charity, incorporated in June 1993.

Figure 5.5: *AI is used to solve problems*

available to solve problems of the world. The sole aim is to provide an ease of access to AI technology which can be used to help people so that it is socially beneficial, fair, accountable, and works for everyone while solving humanitarian and environmental challenges.

Artificial Intelligence provides immense potential to gather, analyze, and combine vast quantities of data from different sources potentially increasing an immense impact on privacy. It is necessary to understand the privacy issue to further counter how to deal with shaping the debate around it.

AI privacy is defined as one's ability to control how our digital data is being stored, modified, and exchanged between different parties. Social agencies like the government and multiple corporations can use different techniques to identify, profile and directly affect one's life without even them knowing about it. With advanced AI algorithms, such fears about these agencies being able to make an impact on your lives, is increasing.

Figure 5.6: *AI Privacy*

Figure 5.7: *AI Privacy*

AI works best with information gathering and computations are done at a good speed which improves data analysis. What sounds scarier is not being able to comprehend how much data devices generate, process, and share which makes us potentially vulnerable to exploitation. AI can track and monitor personal and non-personal data such as keeping track of facial and voice marks for recognition purposes by legal authorities.

Certain sophisticated AI techniques can even predict emotional states of humans while others can deduce political views, sexual orientation, and overall health too. Sometimes, such algorithms also limit access to things like credit, employment and housing services.

Artificial Intelligence: Boon or Bane

AI focuses on data-based approach which uses pattern recognition, image recognition, and speech recognition. All this is possible with human Intelligence which has made the machine to think critically and assist humans in taking very important decisions. The machine is actually using algorithms to give the best matched results based on a lot of data that is entered as input to the machine. There is no doubt that AI technology is helping a lot in human lives for making the life better. But at the same time, if something goes wrong by the machine then who is going to be held responsible? A small mistake can lead to a negative result and potentially create problems.

Figure 5.8: *AI – Boon or Bane*

This could further increase the wedge trust between humans and machines.

Activity 5.2

Let us collate your thoughts about how Artificial Intelligence (inclusion, bias, privacy) is affecting your daily lives in all spheres.

Pros	Cons
• AI machine doesn't get tired even after working 24×7.	• AI technology is costly.
• AI machine can take rational decisions irrespective of gender, religion, and so on.	• AI can lead to increase in unemployment.
• AI can be used in any of the applications like healthcare, security, education, entertainment, transport, and so on.	• AI machine lacks in creativity.
• AI machine gives accurate and fast results based on the input given to the machine.	• AI machine lacks emotions and hence won't understand someone's problem.
• AI machine doesn't need food, water, tea break and can work tirelessly resulting in error-free tasks.	• AI machine is created by a human so there is a possibility of negative impact based on gender bias and prejudice on AI machine.
• AI machines are best suited to work repeated tasks effectively and efficiently.	• Privacy is another issue with AI machines.
• AI machines can assist in your daily routine tasks.	• Legal malpractices.

Balloon Debate

Figure 5.9: *Balloon Debate*

Balloon Debate refers to a debate or sharing of ideas and facts between presenters who debate to win audience approval. The visualization is that of all speakers to be flying in a hot-air balloon which is about to sink. The decision about who should be thrown out so that everyone doesn't die has to be taken. The attempt is to encourage all participants to argue why they shouldn't be thrown out of the balloon.

Activity 5.3

This is a 2-pair activity in a group of 4. You should pen down your observations with regards to AI and its impact to your selected theme; healthcare and argue whether AI plays an important role in the said field. Support with valid arguments and examples.

Theme: Healthcare

How is AI making an impact in the field of the theme selected?

Artificial Intelligence in healthcare has an impact on human lives in number of ways. In the previous section of this chapter, you learned about various approaches in AI. It can be data-based AI or knowledge-based AI. The machine is made intelligent so that it can extract information using algorithms that will function on the data fed into it. It acts like a human brain by just taking a lot of data as input and based on the input, it can process to give the output. The accuracy of output is always dependent on the authenticity of the input collected by that machine. If a lot of data is entered and that is authentic, then there are more chances of getting an accurate result.

Mention some ethical concerns in the field of the selected theme. Give examples to support your statements.

Artificial Intelligence in healthcare is a debatable due to ethical and clinical concerns regarding the patient.

AI machines in healthcare are helpful in number of ways:

- AI can perform any routine and repetitive tasks very easily.
- There is no time bound for AI machines.
- AI machines are more productive.
- AI machines can predict the user's choice and can assist to perform actions as per the requirement.

- AI machines can think logically as per the data input fed into it.
- AI machines can take decisions without prejudice so as not to be taking wrong decisions based on gender, religion, or any other.
- AI can help in maintaining clinical records electronically.

Some of the examples how AI can help in healthcare are as follows:

- AI machine can be used to read the CT scans faster than humans. It can help physicians evaluate patients more efficiently and effectively.
- AI machine can serve better in rural communities.
- AI machine can be used in mining and digging fuels where the human life can be in danger due to hostile.
- AI machines learns from past reports such as X-Ray, CT scan, and MRI to assist doctors regarding diagnosing the problem and then also help in the treatment procedure.
- The IoT-enabled bands help in detecting the problems at early stages.

Mention a few pros and cons of AI inclusion in the field of selected theme.

There are always pros and cons of everything and so it is for Artificial Intelligence too. Some of the intelligent machines might have more advantages than the disadvantages; still there is a fear to use that solution. Everyone thinks that AI will replace humans. People have the perception that if you are going to use AI machines in the healthcare sector, then it is going to replace the surgeons, physicians, nurses, etc. whereas it is not true. The AI machine is trained to do the specific job and assist in the task given to improve the services in the healthcare. For example, if the AI machine is trained to diagnose the disease after reading the CT scan. Then, the intelligent machine is helping the doctor regarding the detection of the disease and guiding for the treatment options.

Pros	Cons
• Able to perform any task endlessly, that is, there is no time limit and the machine doesn't get tired so easily.	• AI-enabled machines are going to increase the budget costs.
• Able to solve problems easily and effectively.	• There are challenges of trust and legal issues.
• Able to handle bulk of information in one go.	• Less human interaction and emotionless.
• Able to convert information into knowledge base to take decisions on it.	• People will be replaced by machine and will further increase unemployment.
• Will help in assisting doctors to take better decision.	• Legal malpractices in case a surgery conducted by arobot go wrong or incorrect inference from an expert system has been implied.
• Patients will be reminded on phones about their appointment schedules, and so on.	
• Every information regarding the patient will be available on one click.	
• Able to do all administrative tasks effectively and efficiently.	

This is an open-ended activity and might have different interpretations. The aforesaid set of observations is one of the interpretations for the Activity 5.3 by the author. You are expected to attempt the next activity as per your research and understanding.

TIP BOT

AI is widely used in the medical field. It is popularly used in identifying potential cancer risks and neurological diseases.

Activity 5.4

This is a 2-pair activity in a group of 4. Collate your observations with regards to AI and its impact to your selected theme such as security, education, entertainment, transport, and service. Conduct a debate on whether AI plays an important role in the said field. Support with valid arguments and examples.

Theme:
How is AI making an impact in the field of the theme selected?
Mention some ethical concerns in the field of the selected theme. Give examples to support your statements.
Mention a few pros and cons of AI inclusion in the field of selected theme.

Pros	Cons

Food for Thought

	It is time to put on your thinking caps and reflect on some thoughts post your readings and observations done so far.
	There is huge replacement of humans with AI-enabled robots in many work spheres, such as physical labor and data analysis. Is it ethical to incorporate AI in such areas to replace human workforce?
	AI-enabled machines and robots will soon be an important part of all workforce. Do you think they will be entitled to sharing incomes paid for such jobs? If yes, how will it be shared?
	Many world problems can be solved with AI inclusion such as food production and preventing hunger and access to clean water and sanitation. Do you think that the benefits will be accessible to all members of the society? If yes, share your views on how to make them available for all.

	Do you think that AI inclusion can be a threat or an advantage keeping in mind how fast technology is progressing and become indispensable parts of your daily lives? ______________________________ ______________________________ ______________________________
	With the advent of AI-enabled technology, more and more people need to be equipped with affordable learning opportunities to keep up with the changing times. Share your views on how to make them accessible to a wider audience. ______________________________ ______________________________ ______________________________
	Humans are making AI-enabled technologies to become smarter. Mention a few ways, by means of which humans can be ahead of Artificial Intelligence. ______________________________ ______________________________ ______________________________

In conclusion, it can be safe to say that it is important to address AI from an ethics, morally, safety, and privacy rights viewpoint. There is a need for a regulatory ethical framework and code of conduct to create a basis for a skilful design, production, and use of AI.

MEMORY BOT

The unique function of AI enables particular handwriting to be read and transform it into an editable text.

TECH BOT

- **Artificial Intelligence:** It is the simulation of human intelligence processes by machines, especially computer systems.
- **AI Access:** It is the privilege or assigned permission to use computer data or resources in some manner.
- **AI Bias:** It is a phenomenon that occurs when an algorithm produces results that are systematically prejudiced due to erroneous assumptions in the machine learning process.

Recap Bot

- The impact of AI on Sustainable Development Goals is to develop responsible citizenship skill as a global concern.
- Ethics can be defined as the study of values, generating moral values for good and bad, right, and wrong.
- Artificial Intelligence is a form of technique with the help of which computers/machines can perform the tasks efficiently and effectively using less time.
- Data-based AI is best suited with pattern recognition, image recognition, and speech recognition.
- Knowledge-based approach works best for expert system where data could be placed in the categories.
- Bias is a phenomenon that occurs when an algorithm produces results that are discriminatory due to the built-in biases created by the programmer.
- AI access can be defined as the mission where world's information can be organized and made available to all.
- AI inclusion suggests making researches, tools, systems and scientific developments available to solve problems.
- The main idea of AI inclusion is to provide an ease of access to AI technology which can help to solve certain common challenges together.
- AI can be used in any of the applications such as healthcare, transport, education, security, entertainment and services.
- AI machine can work tirelessly, take decisions quickly, give accurate results, assist in your daily routines, work best with repetitive tasks and doesn't need food, water, etc. These are some of its advantages.
- AI technology is costly, and it can lead to unemployment, threat to privacy and lacks in creativity and emotions. These are some of its disadvantages.

BRAIN BOT

A. Multiple choice questions.

1. Which one of the following is not an AI ethical concern for humans?

   a. Privacy rights b. Time consumption
   c. Employment d. Costly

2. Which of the following is an advantage of Artificial Intelligence?

   a. Costly b. Creativity
   c. Threat to privacy d. Work tirelessly

3. Which one of the following options is not suitable for AI machines in healthcare?

   a. Learn from past reports and help assisting doctors
   b. Replacing doctors
   c. Can serve better in rural areas
   d. Can help in maintaining clinical records

4. AI bias is also referred as:

   a. Data analysis b. Machine programming
   c. Machine Learning d. Database System

5. AI access can be used for:

   a. World's information to be organized
   b. Information to be universally accessible
   c. Information is useful to all
   d. All of the above

B. Fill in the blanks.

1. ______________ can be defined as the study of values, generating moral values for good and bad, right, and wrong.
2. Knowledge-based approach works best for ______________ systems.
3. Data-based AI is best suited with ______________, ______________ and______________ recognitions.
4. AI ______________ is a phenomenon that occurs when an algorithm produces discriminatory results.

5. AI access can be defined as the mission where information can be made ______________ accessible to all.

6. The impact of AI on SDGs is to develop responsible ______________skill as a global concern.

C. Match the following columns.

	Column A		Column B
1.	Pros of AI	i.	Increase in unemployment
2.	IoT-enabled bands	ii.	Expert system
3.	AI in healthcare	iii.	Pattern, image, and speech recognition
4.	Cons of AI	iv.	Ethics
5.	Lacks emotions	v.	Helps physicians in diagnosis
6.	Data-based AI	vi.	Detects problems in early stages
7.	Knowledge-based approach	vii.	AI machines
8.	Study of values	viii.	Bulk of data with ease, work tirelessly

D. Answer the following questions.

1. Name any scientific researches where ethics plays a major role.
2. Unscramble the following letters to form a word.

   a. CHEIST

   b. CEOOHLGNTY
3. Write any two advantages and disadvantages of Artificial Intelligence.
4. Give any two areas of applications of Artificial Intelligence.
5. Write any two examples of how Artificial Intelligence in healthcare is helpful.
6. Write any two advantages of using Artificial Intelligence in healthcare.
7. Write any two ethical concerns of using Artificial Intelligence.
8. Give any two examples about how Artificial Intelligence is helping in assisting humans in their day-to-day life.
9. Define the terms:

   a. AI Bias b. AI Access c. AI Privacy

Lab Activity

To perform sentence fragmentation online.

1. Visit the link: http://textanalysisonline.com/spacy-sentence-segmentation

   The following screen appears:

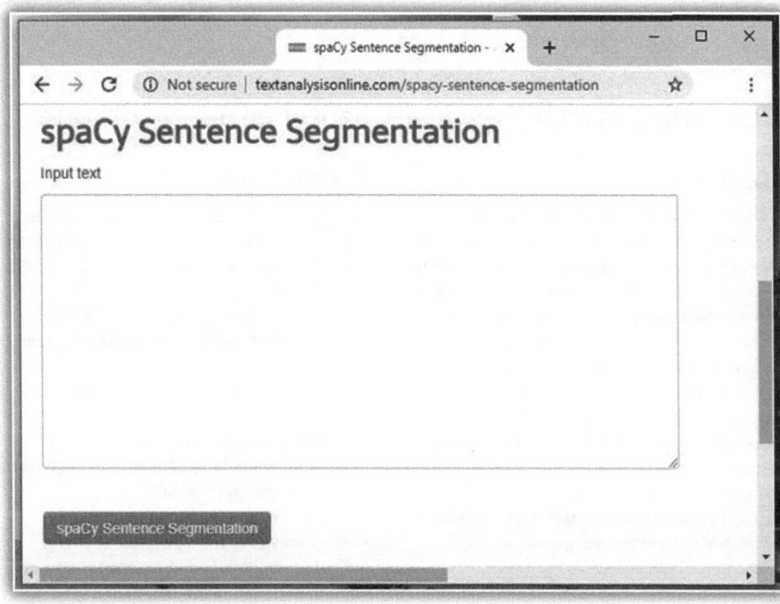

2. Paste the text in the given box:

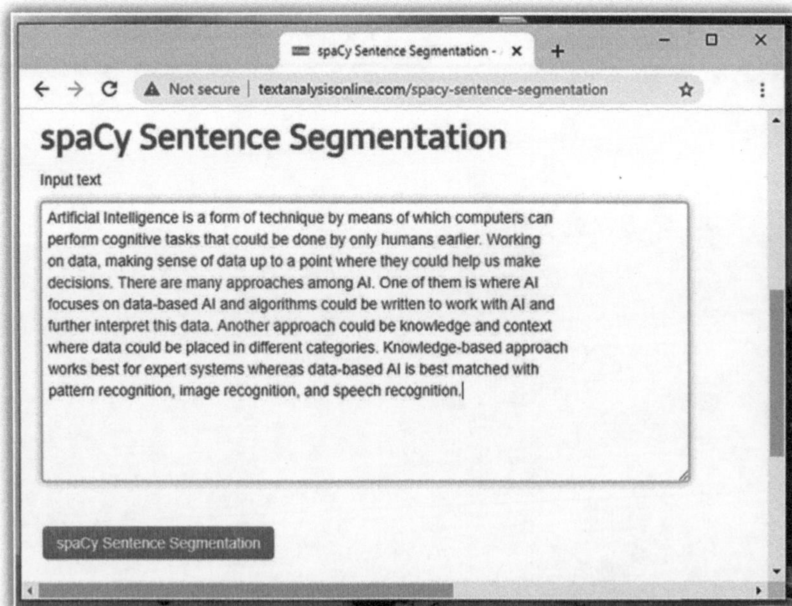

3. Click on **spaCy Sentence Segmentation** button.

4. You will get the following output.

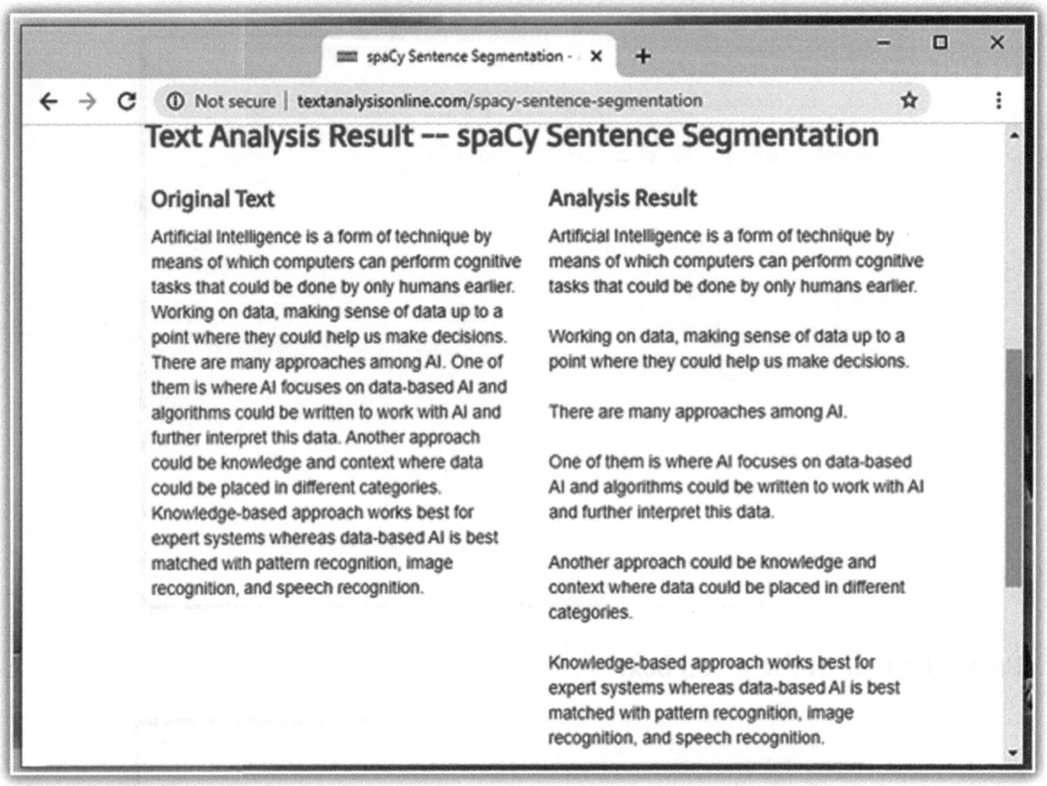

Worksheet

A. State whether the following statements are True or False.

1. Scientists and engineers must find ways on how to handle future projects.
2. Artificial Intelligence ethics is a form of technique by means of which computers can perform cognitive tasks that could be done by only humans earlier.
3. AI bias is referred as Machine Learning bias.
4. Access is used to expand abilities of people so that they can delve into creative spaces and accomplish more in their lives.
5. Privacy provides immense potential to gather, analyze, and combine vast quantities of data from different sources potentially increasing an immense impact on privacy.
6. AI focuses on data-based approach which uses pattern recognition, image recognition, and speech recognition.
7. AI technology is not costly.

B. Fill in the blanks.

1. ________________machines are best suited to work repeated tasks effectively and efficiently.
2. AI in healthcare can be data-based AI or ________________ AI.
3. The accuracy of ______________is always dependent on the authenticity of the input collected by that machine.
4. ________________________is an open-ended activity and might have different interpretations.
5. ____________ suggests making researches, tools, systems and scientific developments available to solve problems.
6. ______________is a form of technique with the help of which computers/machines can perform the tasks efficiently and effectively using less time.

C. Rearrange the following.

1. T I E H C S ________________________
2. P C Y I R A V ________________________
3. A C H M I E N ________________________
4. O T U P T U ________________________

D. Answer the following.

1. Define AI bias.
2. What are the advantages of AI?
3. Write down one example of how AI can help in healthcare.

QUIZ CARD

Multiple choice questions.

1. ________ can track and monitor personal and non-personal data such as keeping track of facial and voice marks for recognition purposes by legal authorities.

   a. AI ☐   b. Ethics ☐
   c. Bias ☐   d. None of these ☐

2. Which is defined as one's ability to control how our digital data is being stored, modified, and exchanged between different parties?

   a. AI ☐   b. Ethics ☐
   c. Bias ☐   d. AI Privacy ☐

3. _______________ can be defined as the mission where world's information can be organized and made universally accessible and useful to all.

   a. AI ☐   b. AI Access ☐
   c. Bias ☐   d. AI Privacy ☐

4. The sole aim of _______________ is to provide an ease of access to AI technology.

   a. AI inclusion ☐   b. AI Access ☐
   c. Bias ☐   d. AI Privacy ☐

5. _______________ approach works best for expert systems.

   a. Data-based ☐   b. Knowledge-based ☐
   c. Both a. and b. ☐   d. None of these ☐

6. _______________ is best matched with pattern recognition, image recognition, and speech recognition.

   a. Data-based ☐   b. Knowledge-based ☐
   c. Both a. and b. ☐   d. None of these ☐

7. ___________ plays a major role in many scientific researches such as stem cell research, cloning/genetically modified food, nuclear technology, animal rights, medical trials, disease research, and biowarfare.

   a. AI ☐   b. Ethics ☐
   c. Bias ☐   d. AI Access ☐

Appendix 1

How to Design a Kahoot?

Kahoot is a game-based learning platform. Kahoots are multiple-choice quiz questions that can be accessed through a web browser or the Kahoot app on a mobile device. The game concept with time-based questions gives the feel of a game show that keeps the players focused. The interface is easy to use so it helps in increasing learning, motivation, concentration, and personalized learning. You can either design a new Kahoot at www.kahoot.com or search for one that is already designed and uploaded in the community.

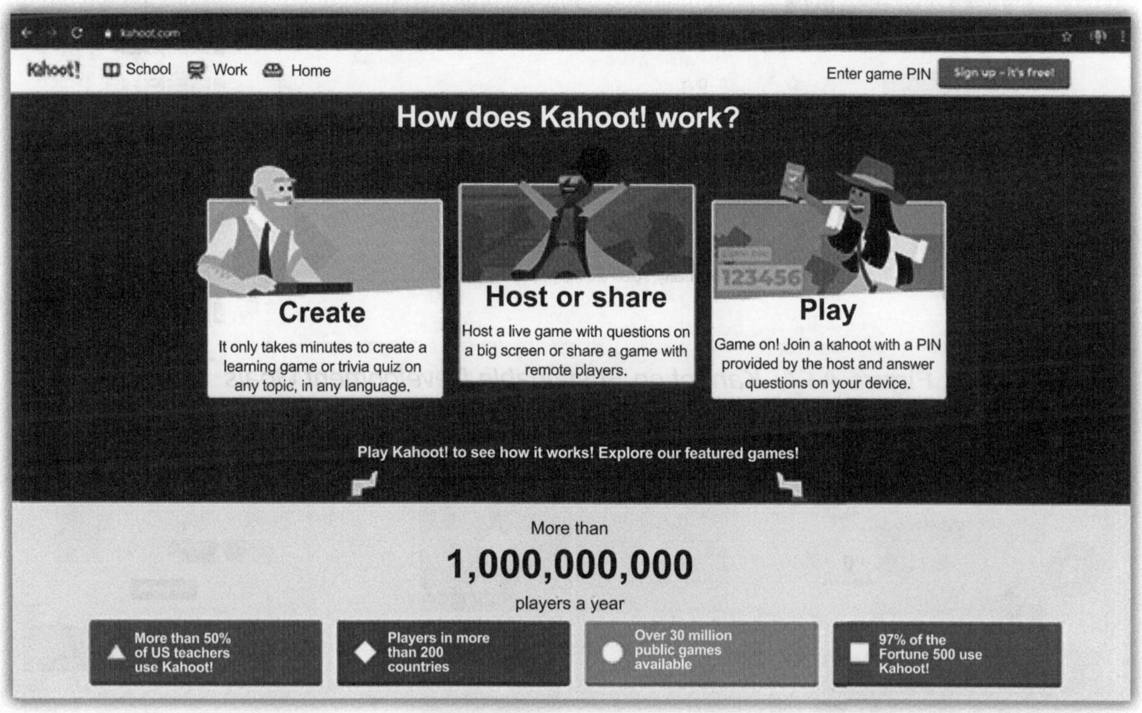

Figure A1.1: *www.kahoot.com*

You can play a game by simply joining in by entering a game pin.

Figure A1.2: *Enter Game Pin*

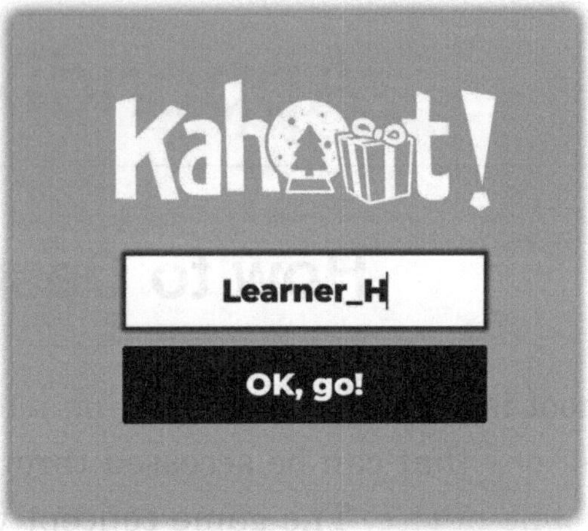

Figure A1.3: *User logged in*

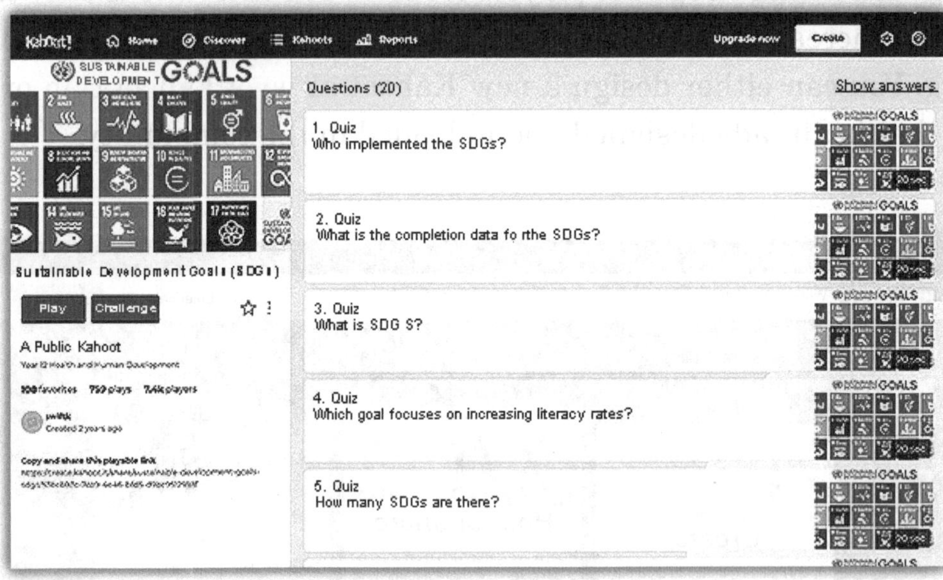

Figure A1.4: *Kahoot on Sustainable Development Goals*

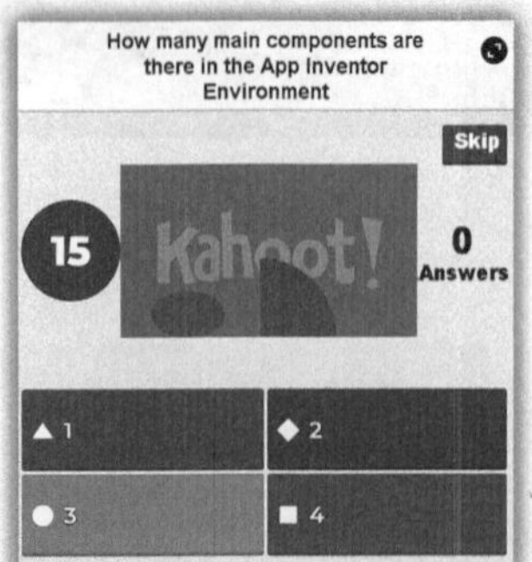

Figure A1.5: *Kahoot Question*

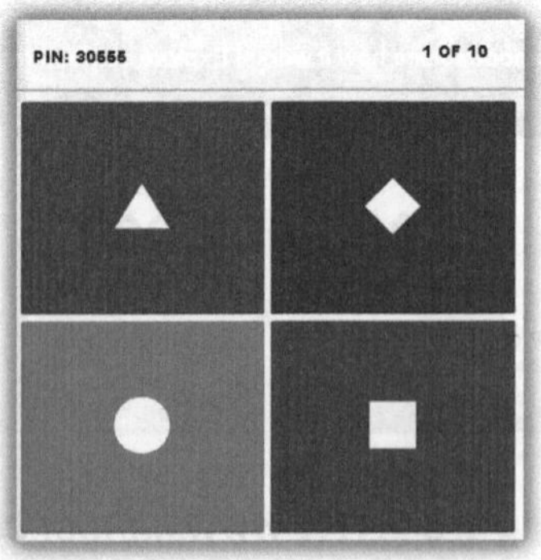

Figure A1.6: *Quiz Choices*

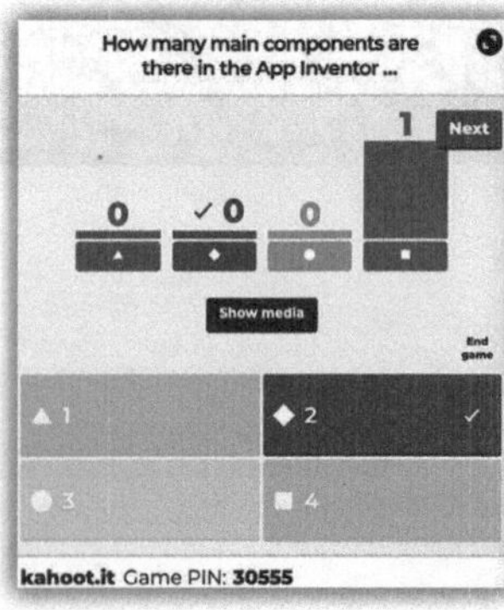

Figure A1.7: *Question Analysis*

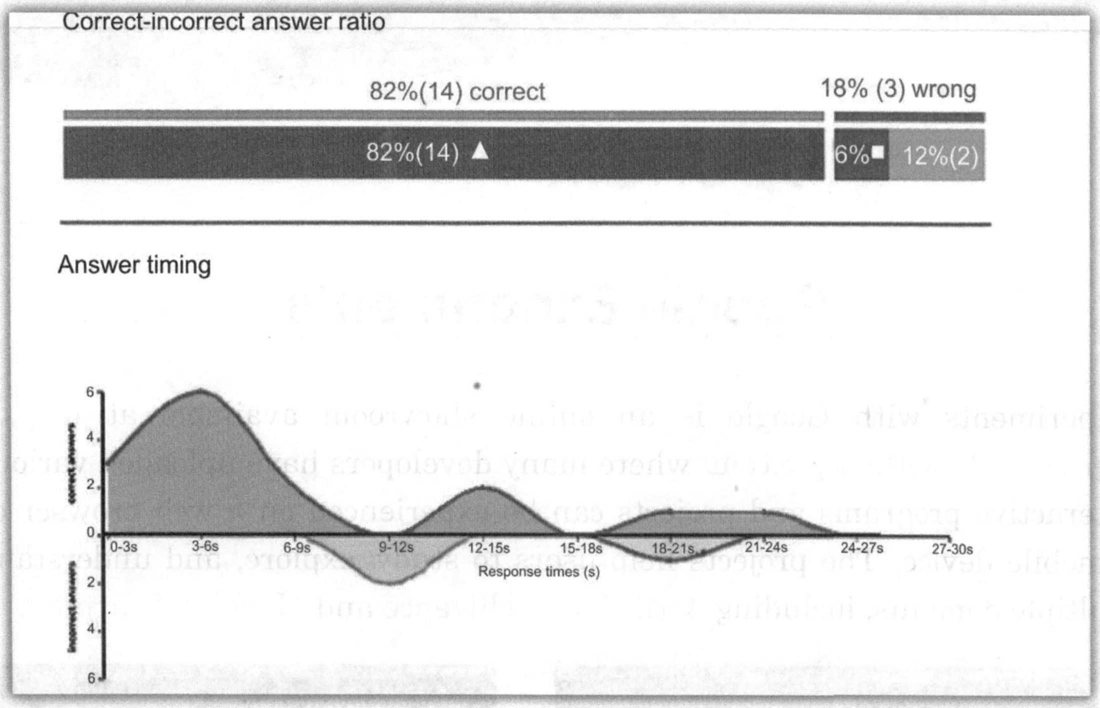

Figure A1.8: *User response analysis*

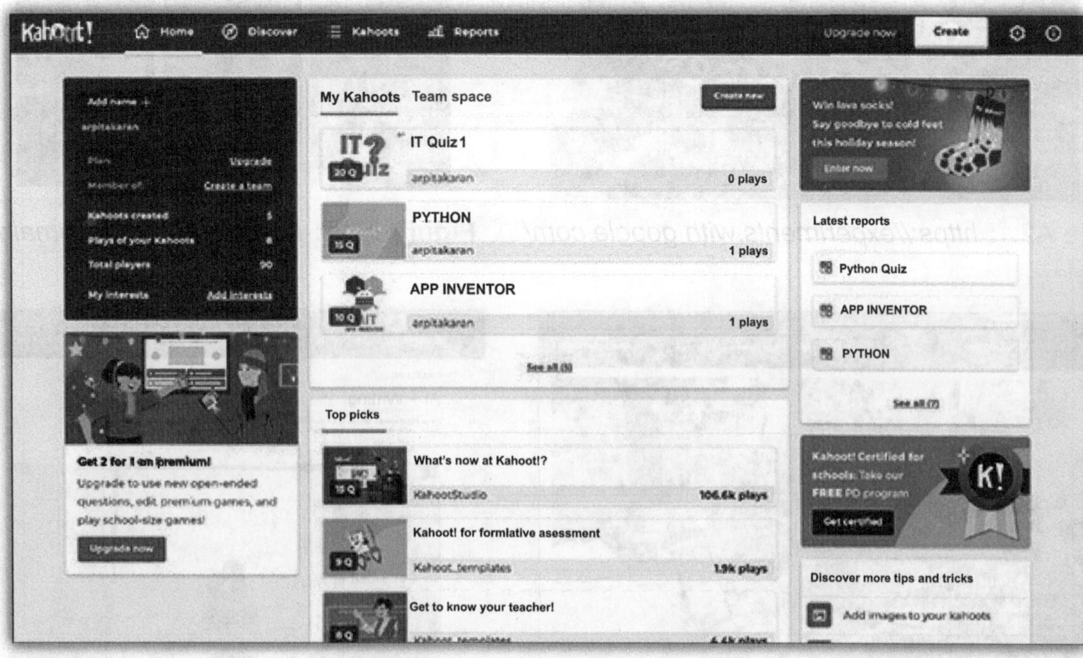

Figure A1.9: *Kahoot User account*

Appendix 2

Google Experiments

Experiments with Google is an online showroom available at https://experiments.withgoogle.com/ where many developers have uploaded various interactive programs and projects can be experienced on a web browser or a mobile device. The projects help users to study, explore, and understand multiple domains, including Artificial Intelligence and Machine Learning.

Figure A2.1: *https://experiments.with google.com/*

Figure A2.2: *Multiple learning domains*

Figure A2.3: *Multiple learning domains*

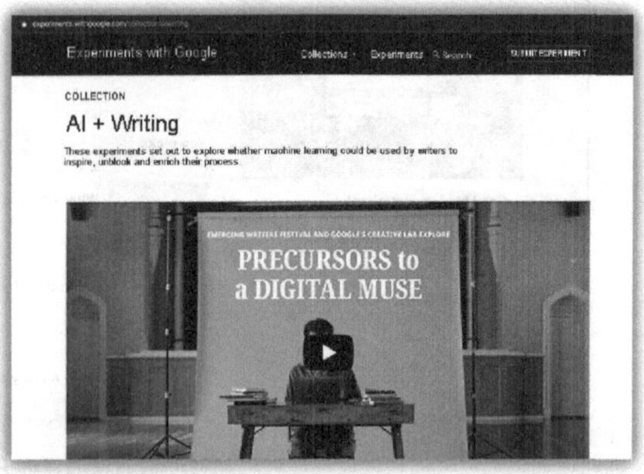

Figure A2.4: *Multiple learning domains*

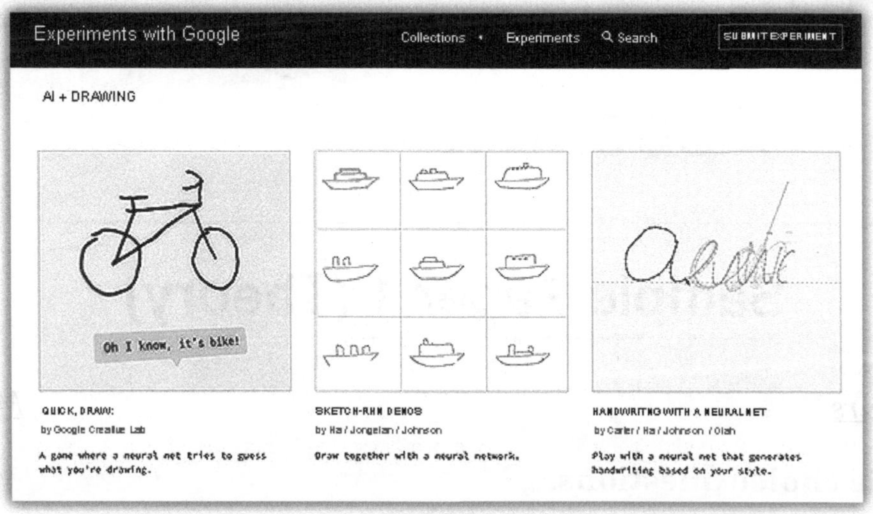

Figure A2.5: *Multiple learning domains*

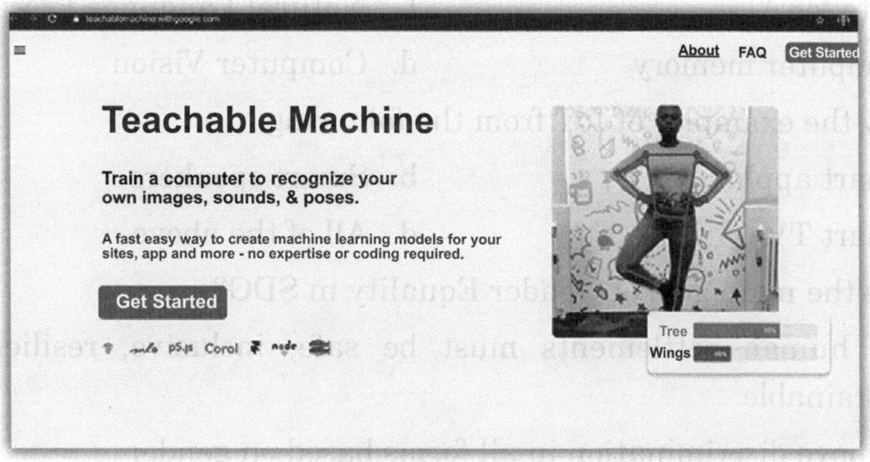

(a)

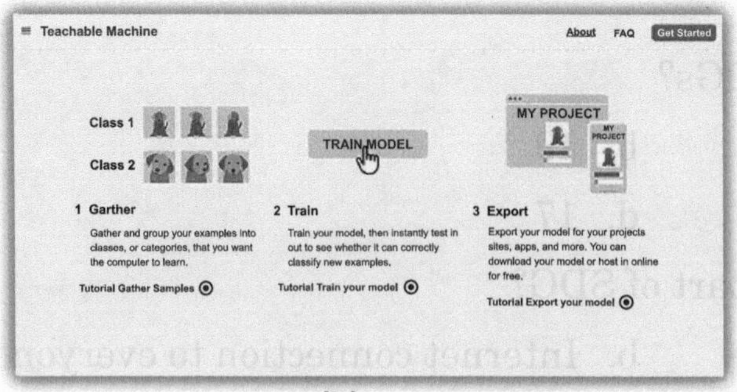

(b)

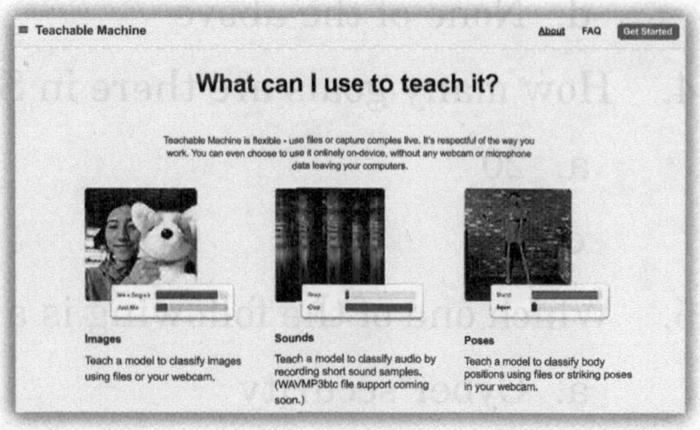

(c)

Figure A2.6: *Teachable Machine*

Appendix 3

Sample Paper 1 (Theory)

Time: 2 hours | *Marks: 50*

A. Multiple choice questions. **½ ×10 =5**

1. Which one of the following is not the pillar of Artificial Intelligence?
   a. Data for AI
   b. Natural Language Processing
   c. Computer memory
   d. Computer Vision
2. Identify the examples of IoT from the following:
   a. Smart appliances
   b. Smart speakers
   c. Smart TV
   d. All of the above
3. What is the main goal of Gender Equality in SDG?
   a. All human settlements must be safe, inclusive, resilient, and sustainable
   b. Remove discrimination in all forms based on gender
   c. Reduce the number of deaths
   d. None of the above
4. How many goals are there in SDGs?
   a. 20
   b. 19
   c. 18
   d. 17
5. Which one of the following is a part of SDG?
   a. Cyber security
   b. Internet connection to everyone
   c. Clean water and sanitation
   d. None of the above

6. The main goal of Narayana Health City in your country around AI theme:
   a. Diagnosing diabetic retinopathy
   b. Pathology
   c. Vertical data analytics centre in-house using Microsoft AI
   d. None of the above
7. The purpose of Ticog Health organization in your country around AI theme:
   a. Pathology b. Dermatology solutions
   c. Breast cancer detection
   d. Cloud-connected ECG devices to detect heart anomalies
8. AI bias is also referred to as:
   a. Database Management System b. Programming
   c. Data analysis d. Machine Learning
9. Which one of the following is suitable for AI machines in transport?
   a. Assist in finding any location
   b. Predicts time taken as per mode of transportation
   c. Suggests different routes
   d. All of the above
10. Communication skills constructively involve:
   a. Observing b. Empathizing
   c. Listening and Speaking d. All of these

B. Fill in the blanks. **½ ×10 =5**

1. ______________ generation of computers is associated with Artificial Intelligence.
2. ______________ is a system of programs and data structures that approximates the operation of the human brain.
3. A Smart Home is also known as ______________.

4. Story Speaker provides two ____________ for writing an interactive story.
5. Displaying compassion and empathy towards society and environment reflects good qualities of a good and ____________ citizen.
6. ____________ is about health and wellness of all beings with ease of access to clean water and sanitation facilities.
7. Smart ____________ on web browser is also based on the user collected data by the AI assistants using data analysis.
8. ____________ skills enhance your ability to accept and relay different kinds of information.
9. ____________ skills are the attributes that are used to effectively interact with one another.
10. ____________ can be defined as the study of values; generating moral values for good and bad, right, and wrong.

C. Match the following. **1×5=5**

Column A	Column B
1. AI was coined by	i. Game to understand the SDG goals
2. Rock, Paper, Scissor	ii. Interactive story
3. Story Speaker	iii. Leadership skills and interpersonal skills
4. Go Goals!	iv. John McCarthy
5. Soft skills	v. Data for AI

D. Answer the following questions.

1. Write full forms for the following. ×3=3
   a. NPC
   b. IoT
   c. K-W-L-H chart

2. Unscramble the following letters to form a word. 1×3=3

   a. ACIPVRY

   b. ACDEIUONT

   c. ACCOMMUNNIIOT

3. Define the following terms with an example: 1×3=3

   a. Computer Vision

   b. Home Automation

   c. AI Privacy

4. Differentiate between the following: 2×2=4

   a. Basic and advanced template of story speaker

   b. Pros and cons of AI inclusion in the field of education

5. What do you understand by Artificial Intelligence? Write any two features about the machine to declare that the machine is acting intelligently. 3

6. What do you understand by Story Speaker? What are the two different ways which are used to write a story in Story Speaker? 3

7. How Artificial Intelligence is used in games? 2

8. Write any two features of a Smart Home. 2

9. How is AI used in the following: 1×2=2

   a. Music and media

   b. Social media feeds

10. Write any two examples of IoT. 2

11. What do you understand by Go Goals? Write the prerequisites for the game. 3

12. Write any three features how Artificial Intelligence is helpful in healthcare. 3

13. Write any four key elements needed for poster making. 2

Sample Paper 1 (Theory)

Marketing Scheme

Time: 2 hours *Marks: 50*

A. Multiple choice questions. **½ ×10 =5**

1. c. Computer memory
2. d. All of the above
3. b. Remove discrimination in all forms based on gender
4. d. 17
5. c. Clean water and sanitation
6. c. Vertical data analytics centre in-house using Microsoft AI
7. d. Cloud-connected ECG devices to detect heart anomalies
8. d. Machine learning
9. d. All of the above
10. d. All of these

B. Fill in the blanks. **½ ×10 =5**

1. Fifth/5th
2. Neural network
3. Home automation
4. Templates
5. Responsible
6. Goal 6/Clean Water and Sanitation
7. Search
8. Communication
9. Soft
10. Ethics

C. Match the following. **1×5=5**

	Column A		Column B
1.	AI was coined by	i.	John McCarthy
2.	Rock, Paper, Scissor	ii.	Data for AI
3.	Story Speaker	iii.	Interactive story
4.	Go Goals!	iv.	Game to understand the SDG goals
5.	Soft skills	v.	Leadership skills and interpersonal skills

D. Answer the following questions.

1. Write full forms for the following. 1×3=3

   a. NPC (Non-Player Characters)

   b. IoT (Internet of Things)

   c. K-W-L-H chart (Know-What-Learn-How chart)

2. Unscramble the following letters to form a word. 1×3=3

   a. ACIPVRY - PRIVACY

   b. ACDEIUONT - EDUCATION

   c. ACCOMMUNNIIOT - COMMUNICATION

3. Define the following terms with an example: 1×3=3

   ½ mark for definition and ½ mark for any example

   a. Computer Vision

   b. Home Automation

   c. AI Privacy

4. Differentiate between the following:

   1 mark for each correct difference 2×2=4

   a. Basic and advanced template of story speaker

   b. Pros and cons of AI inclusion in the field of education

5. What do you understand by Artificial Intelligence? Write any two features about the machine to declare that the machine is acting intelligently.

   1 mark for definition of AI and 1 mark for each correct feature

6. What do you understand by Story Speaker? What are the two different ways which are used to write a story in Story Speaker?

   1 mark for defining story speaker. 1 mark for each correct way to write story in Story Speaker. 3

7. How Artificial Intelligence is used in games?

   1 mark for any use of AI in gaming 2

8. Write any two features of a Smart Home.

   1 mark for any one correct feature of a smart home 2

9. How is AI used in the following:

   a. Music and media

   b. Social media feeds

   1 mark for any one correct use of AI in the areas given 1×2=2

10. Write any two examples of IoT.

    1 mark for each correct example of IoT 2

11. What do you understand by Go Goals? Write the prerequisites for the game.

    1 mark for Go Goals definition. ½ mark for each correct prerequisite for the game (minimum 4 required) 3

12. Write any three features how Artificial Intelligence is helpful in healthcare.

    1 mark for each correct feature of AI that is helpful in healthcare 3

13. Write any four key elements needed for poster making.

    ½ mark for each correct key element for designing poster 2

Sample Paper 2 (Theory)

Time: 2 hours | *Marks: 50*

A. Multiple choice questions. **½ ×10 =5**

1. Which one of the following is not an example of AI-based Chatbot?
   a. Siri b. Google Chrome
   c. Alexa d. Google Assistant
2. Story Speaker is:
   a. Google Application b. Tool to create interactive stories
   c. Easy to use without any knowledge of coding
   d. All of the above
3. What is the aim of No Poverty Goal in SDG?
   a. Remove discrimination in all forms based on gender
   b. Economic growth, higher levels of productivity with technological innovations
   c. Poverty must be finished in all its forms from everywhere
   d. All of the above
4. By when the agenda of SDGs is to be achieved:
   a. 2030 b. 2020
   c. 2021 d. 2029
5. AI algorithms are working in the background to help users in suggesting after analysis and predictions:
   a. False b. True
   c. Can't say d. None is mentioned
6. The purpose of cure skin organization in your country around AI theme:
   a. Pathology b. Dermatology solutions
   c. Breast cancer detection d. None of the above
7. A responsible citizen of the country is expected to be:
   a. Caring b. Conscientious
   c. Contributing member of the society
   d. All of the above

8. Which one of the following is suitable for AI machines in healthcare:
   a. Learn from past reports and help assisting doctors
   b. Can serve better in rural areas
   c. Can help in maintaining clinical records
   d. All of the above
9. Research skills help in:
   a. Data collection
   b. Planning and scheduling
   c. Both a. and b.
   d. None of these
10. Communication skills constructively build:
   a. Verbal
   b. Visual
   c. Written
   d. All of these

B. Fill in the blanks. **½ ×10 =5**

1. ____________ is an Artificial Intelligence software/program that simulates a conversation with a human being.
2. ____________ is the domain of Artificial Intelligence which is capable of communication between people and machines.
3. Story Speaker is an add-on tool by ____________.
4. Smart City is a ____________ city which uses IoT to provide better quality of life to everyone.
5. The three pillars of SDGs are economic, environmental, and____________.
6. ____________ aims to correct the imbalance by ensuring that all have access to affordable, reliable, and enhanced modern energy services.
7. Artificial Intelligence ____________ are working in the background all the time for suggesting online purchases and bookings.
8. Communication skills involve observing, empathizing, adapting, listening and ____________ to build verbal, visual and written communication.

9. AI enabled smart _____________ can listen, understand, learn, and perform administrative tasks.
10. AI _____________ suggests making researches, tools, systems, and scientific developments available to solve problems.

C. Match the following. 1×5=5

Column A	Column B
1. Computer vision	i. IoT
2. Google Home	ii. Collect data and critically analyze from different sources
3. Smart City	iii. Emoji Scavenger Hunt
4. Research skill	iv. Costly
5. AI technology	v. Smart Speaker

D. Answer the following questions.

1. Write full forms for the following. 1×3 =3
   a. NLP
   b. TREWS
   c. AI
2. Unscramble the following letters to form a word. 1×3 =3
   a. EROYVPT
   b. AABEISSTNLU
   c. AEECHSRR
3. Define the following terms with an example. 1×3=3
   a. Data for AI
   b. Poster
   c. AI bias
4. Differentiate between the following: 2×2=4
   a. Soft skills and technical skills
   b. Pros and cons of AI inclusion in the field of healthcare

5. Name three domains of AI and also write one example for each. 3

6. Define Story Speaker. Also, write any two elements of the Story Speaker template.

7. What is the role of Artificial Intelligence in SDG? 2

8. Write any two features of a Smart Home and Smart City. 2

9. How is AI used in the following: 1×2=2

   a. Online Ads Network

   b. Security and Surveillance

10. What do you understand by IoT? 2

11. Write the purpose of the following while playing game Go Goals: 3

    a. Board

    b. Token

    c. Question sheets

12. Write any three features how Artificial Intelligence is helpful in education. 3

13. What do you understand by a poster? Explain it with the help of an example. 2

Sample Paper 3 (Theory)

Time: 2 hours *Marks: 50*

A. Multiple choice questions. **½ ×10 =5**

1. Google home is a:
   a. Story Speaker b. Web browser
   c. Google Assistant d. Smart speaker
2. Story Speaker is:
   a. Google Assistant b. Application by Google
   c. Google Chrome d. Search engine
3. Many countries committed for taking actions to meet the SDGs by 2030:
   a. True b. False
   c. Can't say d. None is mentioned
4. Which one of the following is a pillar of SDG?
   a. Economic b. Social
   c. Environment d. All of the above
5. AI algorithms plays a very important role in:
   a. Collecting the data all the time
   b. Analyzing the data collected
   c. Predicting and suggesting the user
   d. All of the above
6. The purpose of Niramai organization in your country around AI theme:
   a. Pathology b. Dermatology solutions
   c. Breast cancer detection d. None of the above
7. Which one of the following is an AI ethical concern for humans?
   a. Privacy rights b. Time consumption
   c. Working hours d. None of the above

8. Which one of the following is suitable for AI machines in entertainment:
   a. Learn from your previous searches
   b. Suggestions as per your previous actions
   c. Collects data from users
   d. All of the above
9. Research can be done using:
   a. Internet
   b. Articles
   c. Surveys
   d. All of the above
10. Communication skills enhance the following ability:
    a. Accept information
    b. Relay different kinds of information
    c. Both a. and b.
    d. None of these

B. Fill in the blanks. **½ x10 =5**

1. _____________ is the study of how the language sounds.
2. The main goal of a Smart City is to provide better _____________ of life to every individual.
3. The dream of Home Automation wouldn't be possible without the use of _____________ and _____________ connectivity.
4. The _____________ adopted the SDGs agenda to achieve 17 goals by 2030.
5. _____________ encourages entrepreneurship and job creation with technological innovations.
6. Research skill helps to _____________ data and critically analyze information from different sources.
7. AI is augmenting human beings and machines to work _____________ to change the face of any kind of industry.
8. _____________ skills are the attributes and knowledge required to perform a particular task.

9. The main idea of AI inclusion is to provide an ease of access to AI technology which can help to solve certain common __________ together.

C. Match the following. **1×5=5**

Column A	Column B
1. Mystery Animal	i. Ability to make others understand what do you want to say
2. Smart Home	ii. Project management and Data analysis
3. Communication skill	iii. Healthcare, transport, and education
4. Technical skills	iv. Home that works on automation which is safe and secure
5. AI applications	v. Natural Language Processing

D. Answer the following questions.

1. Write full forms for the following. 1×3 =3

   a. IoT b. SDG c. UN

2. Unscramble the following letters to form a word. 1×3 =3

   a. ALITEHC b.AEHHLT c.EEVINNNMORT

3. Define the following terms with an example: 1×3=3

   a. Natural Language Processing

   b. Research

   c. AI access

4. Differentiate between the following: 2×2=4

   a. Soft skills and technical skills

   b. Pros and cons of AI inclusion in the field of transport

5. Name any two AI assistants. Also, write any four ways how these AI help us in your daily lives. 3

6. What do you understand by Story Speaker? Write any three prerequisite for story speaker. 3
7. Write any two ethical concerns of using Artificial Intelligence. 2
8. Write any four parameters that declares a city as a Smart City. 2
9. How is AI used in the following: 1×2=2
   a. Navigation and travel
   b. Smartphones
10. What do you understand by an interactive story? 2
11. Name the website for Go-Goals!! game and materials needed to play this game. 3
12. Write any three features how Artificial Intelligence is helpful in transport. 3
13. What do you understand by technical skills? Write any two technical skills. 2

Appendix 4

Chapter-wise Solutions

Chapter 1

Brain Bot

A. Multiple choice questions.

1. b. Making a machine intelligent
2. c. Speaking
3. b. Neural network
4. d. Anthropomorphism
5. b. John McCarthy
6. d. Natural Language Processing
7. a. Chatbot
8. b. Natural Language Processing
9. a. Fifth
10. d. Phonology

B. Fill in the blanks.

1. Applications	2. See	3. Rock, paper, scissor
4. Robotics	5. Drones	6. Pattern

C. Match the following.

Column A	Column B
1. Chatbots	iii. Siri, Alexa
2. Applications of AI	v. Self-driving cars, chatbots
3. Mystery Animal	ii. NLP
4. Programming Language used in AI	i. Python, Lisp
5. Emoji Scavenger Hunt	iv. Computer Vision

Chapter 2

Brain Bot

A. Multiple choice questions.

1. a. Home Automation
2. d. A home that works on automation which is safe and secure
3. d. All of the above
4. a. Yes
5. b. No
6. d. All of the above
7. a. Yes
8. c. Google
9. d. All of the above
10. c. Cortana

B. Fill in the blanks.

1. Smartphones, internet connectivity
2. Internet
3. Quality
4. Story Speaker
5. Voice
6. Templates

C. Match the following.

Column A	Column B
1. AI Assistants	iii. Alexa, Cortana
2. Story Speaker	v. Google add-on
3. Smart Home	iv. IoT
4. Google Home	i. Smart Speaker
5. Gmail	ii. Google E-mail

Chapter 3

Brain Bot

A. Multiple choice questions.

1. b. Sustainable Development Goals
2. d. 17
3. b. End poverty in all its form from everywhere
4. c. Provision of Internet to all
5. b. Goal 4 – Quality Education, Goal 5 – Gender Equality and Goal 10 – Reduced Inequalities

6. d. Halt the use of biotechnology and genetic engineering
7. a. They are a legally binding international treaty that all nations are required to follow
8. c. 2030
9. c. Countries in Asia
10. d. None of the above

B. Fill in the blanks.

1. United Nations, 17
2. Responsible
3. 2030
4. Compassion, empathy
5. Insights, understand/ learn
6. Everywhere
7. Climate, Climate Action
8. Oceans
9. Degradation, loss, land
10. Below water
11. Integral
12. Rules

C. Match the following.

Column A	Column B
1. SDG	iii. Sustainable Development Goals
2. The quality of the environment along with reducing number of deaths	v. Good health and well-being
3. Discrimination in all forms based on gender	i. Gender equality
4. Go Goals!	vi. Game
5. All human settlements must be safe, inclusive, resilient, and sustainable	iv. Sustainable cities and communities
6. Economic growth, higher levels of productivity with technological innovations	ii. Decent work and economic growth

D. Answer the following questions.

2. Unscramble the following letters to form a word.
   a. OASCLI - SOCIAL
   b. USSENTLAAIB - SUSTAINABLE

Chapter 4

Brain Bot

A. Multiple choice questions

1. b. Time consuming
2. d. Diagnosing diabetic retinopathy
3. b. Pathology
4. c. Data Analysis
5. b. Targeted Real-Time Early Warning Score

B. Fill in the blanks.

1. Data analysis
2. Algorithms, bookings
3. Data analysis
4. Data, sources
5. Communication
6. Listen, learn
7. Communication
8. Qure.ai
9. Tricog Health

C. Match the following.

1. Soft Skill	vii. Teamwork
2. Smart Search on web	i. Data analysis
3. Technical Skill	iv. Project management
4. Communication Skill	ii. Speaking
5. Digital assistant	iii. Chatbot
6. Niramai	viii. Breast cancer detection
7. Cure skin	vi. Dermatology solutions
8. Research Skill	v. Collect data and critically analyze from different sources

D. Answer the following questions.

2. Unscramble the following letters to form a word.

   a. IKSLL – SKILL   b. ACEESHRR - RESEARCH

Chapter 5

Brain Bot

A. Multiple choice questions.

1. b. Time consumption
2. d. Work tirelessly
3. b. Replacing doctors
4. c. Machine Learning
5. d. All of the above

B. Fill in the blanks.

1. Ethics 2. Expert 3. Pattern, image and speech

4. Bias 5. Universally 6. Citizenship

C. Match the following.

Column A		Column B
1. Pros of AI	viii.	Bulk of data with ease and work tirelessly
2. IoT-enabled bands	vi.	Detects problems in early stages
3. AI in healthcare	v.	Helps physicians in diagnosis
4. Cons of AI	i.	Increase unemployment
5. Lacks emotions	vii.	AI machines
6. Data-based AI	iii.	Pattern, image, and speech recognition
7. Knowledge based approach	ii.	Expert system
8. Study of values	iv.	Ethics

D. Answer the following questions.

2. Unscramble the following letters to form a word:

   a. CHEIST - ETHICS

   b. CEOOHLGNTY - TECHNOLOGY

Appendix 5

Co-curricular Activities

Practical: 50 marks

List of activities that can be assessed under co-curricular activities for the practical component.

The following activities from the content can be assessed under co-curricular activities:

S No.	Activity	Chapter No. and Name	Activity No.
I.	Write a letter to your future self, mentioning what you have learned about Artificial Intelligence and what are the skills you would like to learn and acquire for availing futuristic job opportunities.	Chapter 1: Motivate with AI	Activity 1.13
II.	Kahoot Quiz: Conduct an online Kahoot quiz on AI concepts.	Chapter 1: Motivate with AI	Appendix 1
III.	Story Speaker activity: To write an interactive story using the Google Doc extension of Story Speaker.	Chapter 2: Motivate with AI	Activity 2.5
IV.	Kahoot online quiz/Pen paper Quiz: Sustainable Development Goals	Chapter 3: Purpose with AI	Appendix 1
V.	Job Advertisement Poster Making: Create a poster for a job advertisement	Chapter 4: Possibilities with AI	Activity 4.4
VI.	Balloon Debate: Conducting a balloon debate wherein the teams talk in favor of Al and against Al relating it to various domains like agriculture, transport, security, etc.	Chapter 5: Al Ethics with AI	Activity 5.3